Piers and Seaside Towns: An Artist's Journey

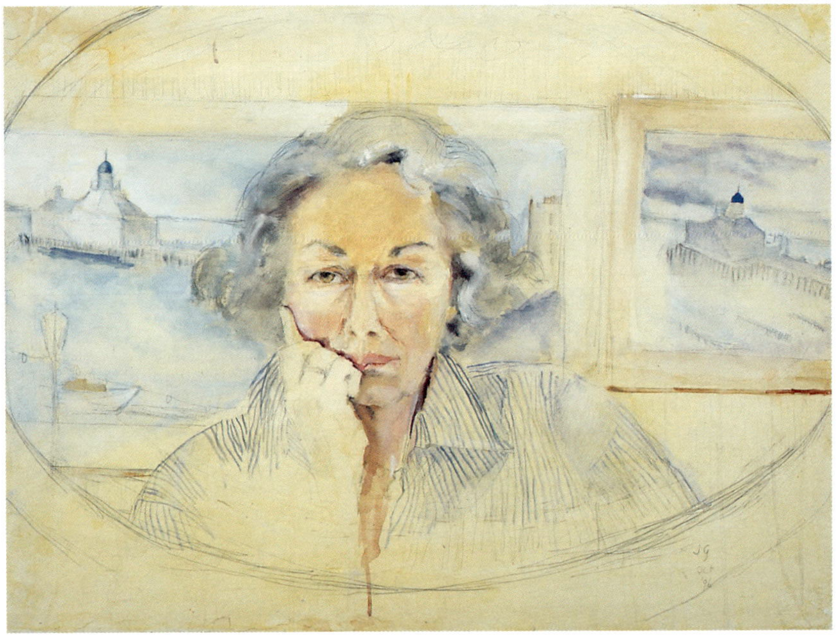

Piers and Seaside Towns:
An Artist's Journey

Judith Greenbury

Sansom & Company

First published in 2001
SANSOM & COMPANY
81g Pembroke Road, Bristol BS8 3EA

Telephone: 0117 9737207
Fascimile: 0117 9238991

ISBN 1 900178 63 X

British Cataloguing-in-Publication Data
A catalogue record for this book is available from the British Library.

Typeset by Mayhew Typesetting, Rhayader, Powys and
Printed by Hackman Print Group, South Wales

CONTENTS

ACKNOWLEDGEMENTS

I owe much to the friends who accompanied me on my single-minded journeys to the sea: to Angela Searle, Carol Giles, Janie Bright and my niece Debbie Gibberd.

And to Mr Hobbs, who drove my little car, north and south, from coast to coast, and always with such good humour.

For the evocative photographs of the piers in their heyday, I am indebted to Martin Easdown and Linda Sage (Marlinova Collection). I wish also to thank Matthew Parris and *The Times* for permission to reproduce part of his article on the West Pier, Brighton.

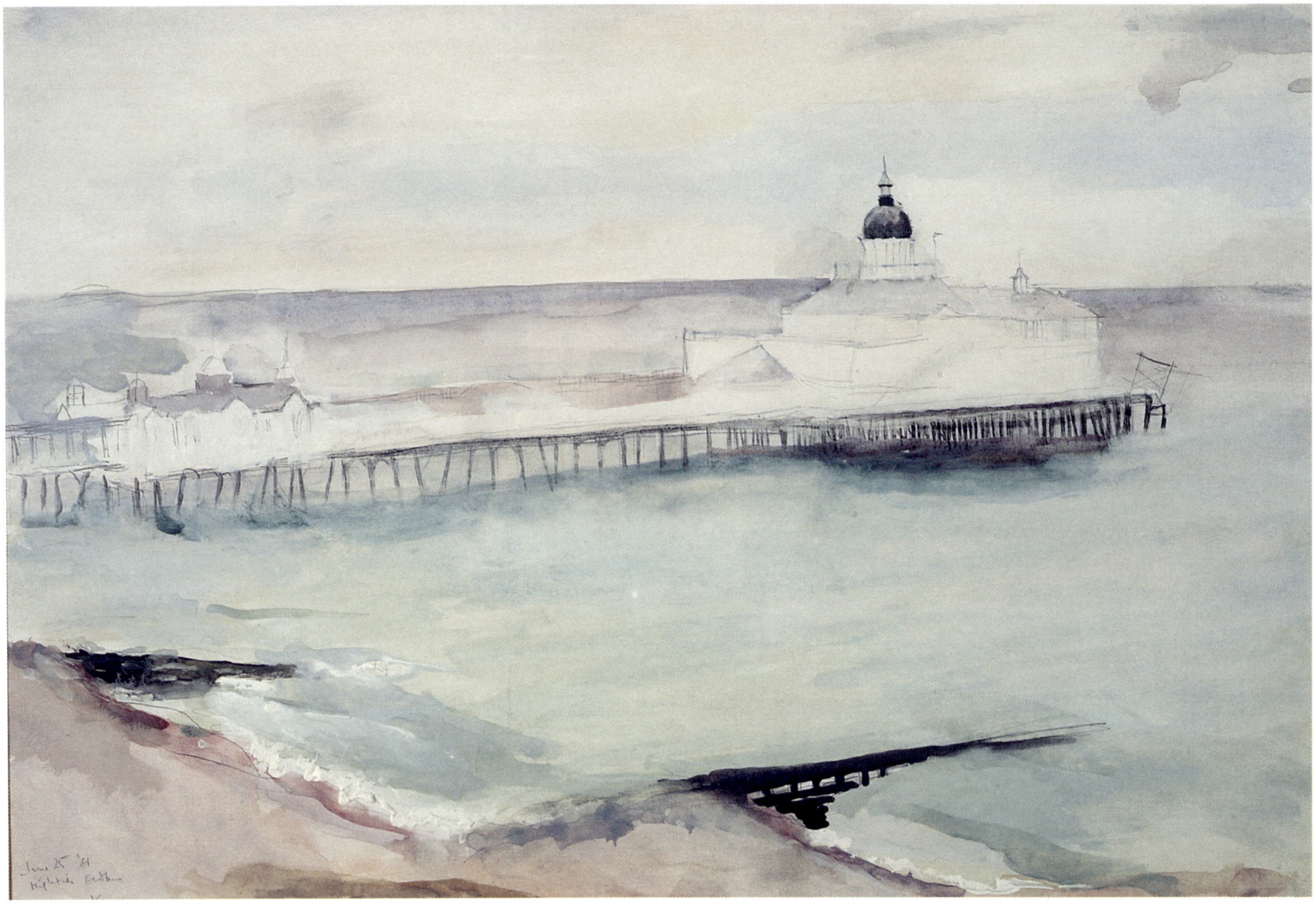

Eastbourne Pier.

EASTBOURNE – MY FIRST PIER

It may seem strange that a book about piers and seaside towns should open with two paragraphs about croquet, but it was my husband's passion for croquet that took me to these seaside towns in the first place and gave me the time, and opportunity, to paint them.

One of our first croquet matches was in Eastbourne. It was a cold April, and our hotel room was bleak, but beyond the window I could see the pier, lapped by a pale green sea. It was high tide, and I knew then what I wanted to do, what I wanted to paint.

Association croquet, for a non-player, is not exciting. It is, in truth, rather a boring game to watch: just one player on the lawn at a time, the opponent sitting out waiting for a breakdown of play and his turn to go on. If the play is good and the 'breaks' go well, hoop after hoop taken, it can be exciting, but that is rare and the uninformed spectator gets lost. One afternoon, after watching my husband stalking around the lawn in his characteristic habit, his fine head bent down, kicking the turf as he went, furious at messing up a perfectly good, and promising, break, I decided he did not need me there; in fact, he would probably rather I did not watch when his play was not going well. I would go off and paint, I would paint the seaside, the houses and, where there was a pier, I would paint the pier. I would now actually look forward to away matches, for good croquet clubs are often situated in seaside towns. We were then in Eastbourne and so that town's particularly lovely pier was the first that I painted.

So began this series of paintings and drawings, started during my husband's life time and, after the appalling shock of his final illness and his untimely death, I had a reason to go away, to have holidays with a purpose, a series of paintings to start, to look forward to, to enjoy.

It was at Eastbourne that I first noticed the magic of that extraordinary structure built out into the sea: the bright blue-green dome topping the 'Eastern' pavilion, finishing the pier, making a wonderful subject. The Eastbourne Pier Company was formed in 1865, the pier designed by the great Eugenius Birch, and the first pile driven in on April 18th, 1866. The pier was officially opened by Lord Edward Cavendish on June 13th, 1870, although work on the 1,000-foot pier, landing stage, kiosk and windbreak was not completed for another two years. Appallingly, on New Year's Day, 1877, a wild storm washed away the shore end and the pier had to be rebuilt at a higher level.

The first, 400-seat, theatre was constructed for just £250 at the seaward end in 1888 and eleven years later was replaced by a 1,000-seat theatre. A new landing stage was built, and two saloons were put up mid-way along the pier. New entrance buildings were added and in 1925 a 900-seat music pavilion was built at the shore end.

After Brighton's West Pier, Eastbourne is probably Birch's finest pier and although war, fire and storms have battered it, it still stands, is very much alive, and is now lit up at night. In 1997, it was voted 'Pier of the Year' by members of the National Piers Society.

After the initial excitement of painting the sea – its changing colours of deep blue or purple on the horizon, the pale green going to white of the sea nearer the shore – after painting the sea coming in round the iron structure of the pier, lapping the stanchions, and the 'Eastern' pavilion with its lovely egg-shaped cupola (always difficult to draw its exact shape) at the seaward end, and the two little pavilions further

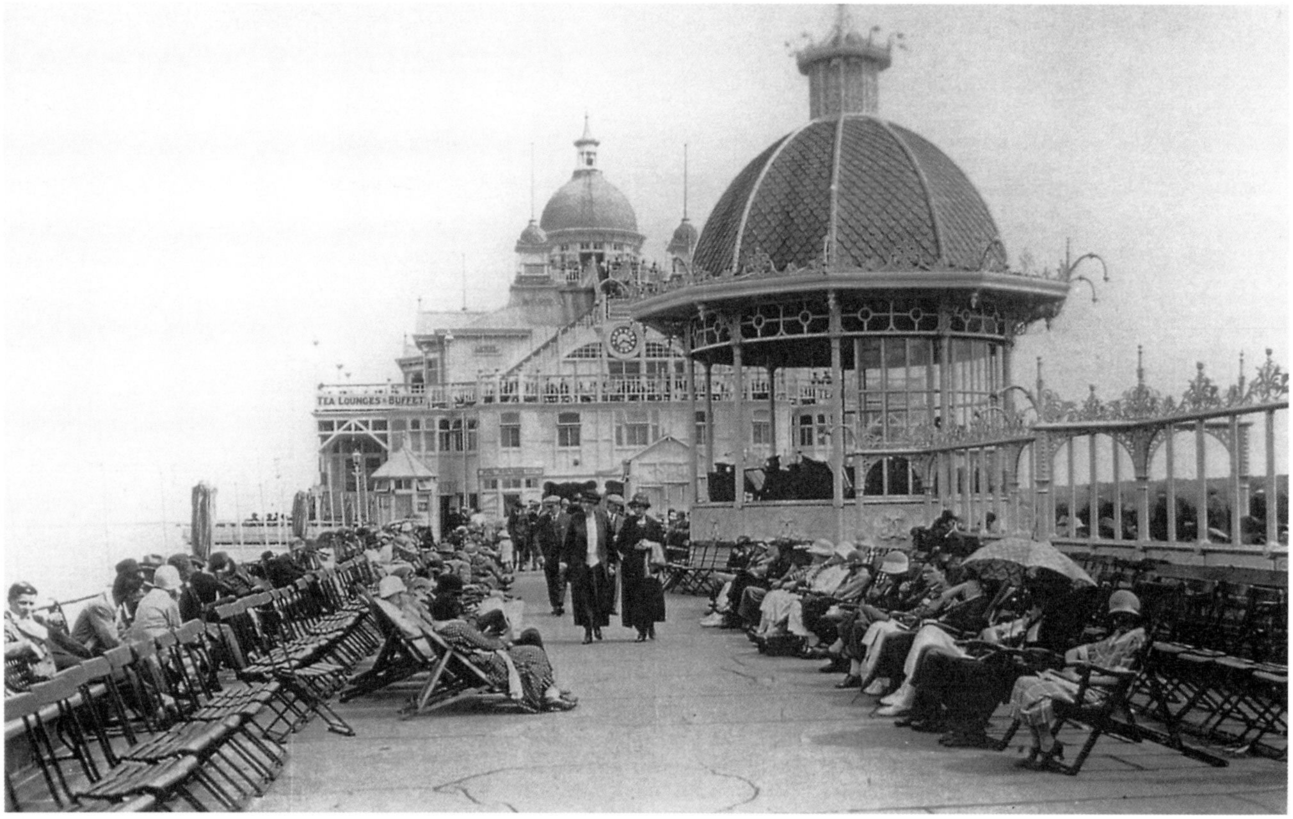

Eastbourne Pier, 1920s.

down with the large silver domed building near the shore – after drawing and painting this, there is always an awkward decision to be made. Should I draw in and paint the cast iron screw piles that hold the pier up, should I draw them in carefully, or just paint a dark pattern? It is so difficult, for if you do it really carefully, you get very interested in the structure and notice how the pairings of the legs go and how they are in perspective so that you have, perhaps, two legs and then two legs, and then four legs getting smaller and smaller until eventually there is a great complicated iron structure holding the main building up with cross-bars and bits of metal stuck in at all angles. Do you put all that in? And then this dark mass dominates the composition and it is not at all what you had originally intended to paint, for the ethereal magic of the picture disappears in the strong detail.

So to begin with I often got lost, and fascinated, and put it all in carefully. But then looking at the whole composition and hanging on to what I originally found exciting, I would put the painting in the bath, and since I am using water-colour I would, with my tooth mug, take out the darkness of the complicated structure by pouring water over it all until the picture balanced and the iron structure was less obtrusive.

Painting, for me, is so often putting in and taking out: rather like 'Tonking', the method the great teacher, Henry Tonks, taught at The Slade when he would cover a day's oil painting with tissue paper, blot it hard and, taking the tissue paper off, leave just an echo of the day's work. It is commonly thought that you cannot do this with water-colour; that once in, it has to be left, but this is a fallacy. All you need is a good strong hand-made paper, which you can treat fairly roughly as Turner did, often putting his paintings in water to get the effects he wanted. It works, it really works, although occasionally the paper, horrifyingly, goes through and you have a hole or a very thin skin left. Painting is never the easy, happy, relaxed 'hobby' that so many of the general public think it is. It is truly exciting, often hair-raising: it makes you really look, and I don't know any excitement to equal the thrill of having 'seen' a picture and then getting it down on paper.

For several years we went twice a year to Eastbourne. We always stayed at the same hotel, a tall grey Victorian building, which was named after one of the Duke of Devonshire's houses for, I believe, he once owned much of Eastbourne. It was not luxurious, but it had a

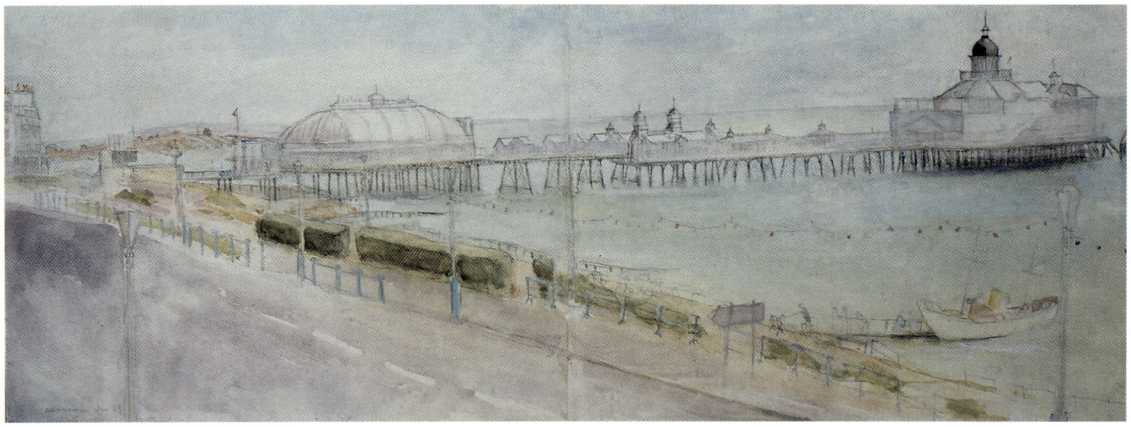

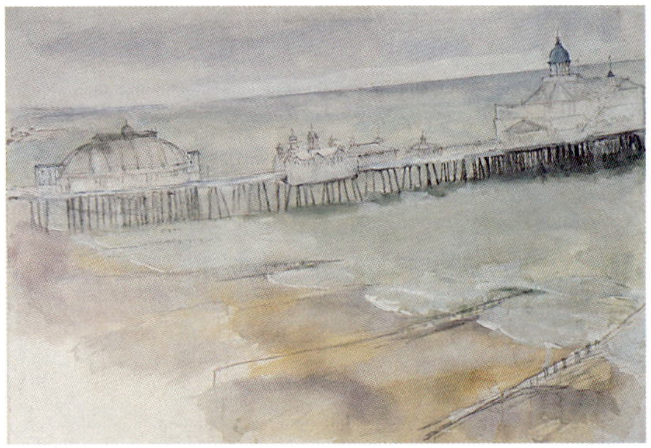

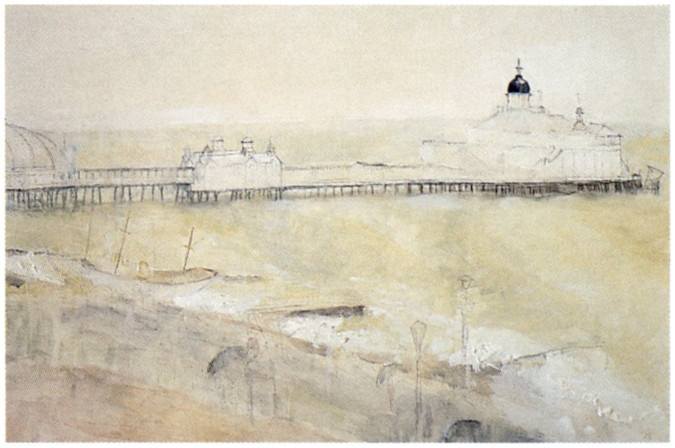

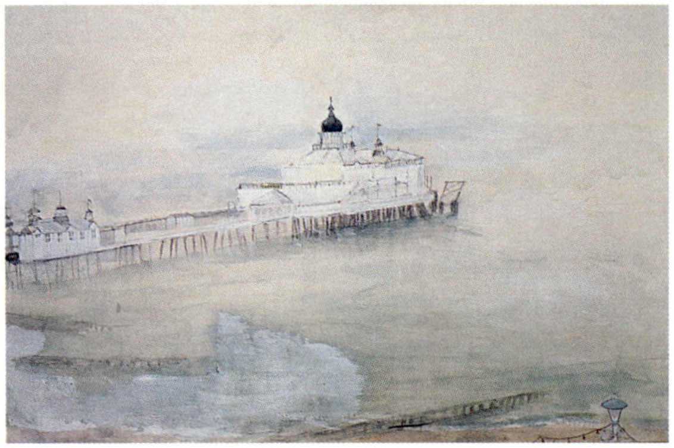

Paintings of Eastbourne Pier from hotel.

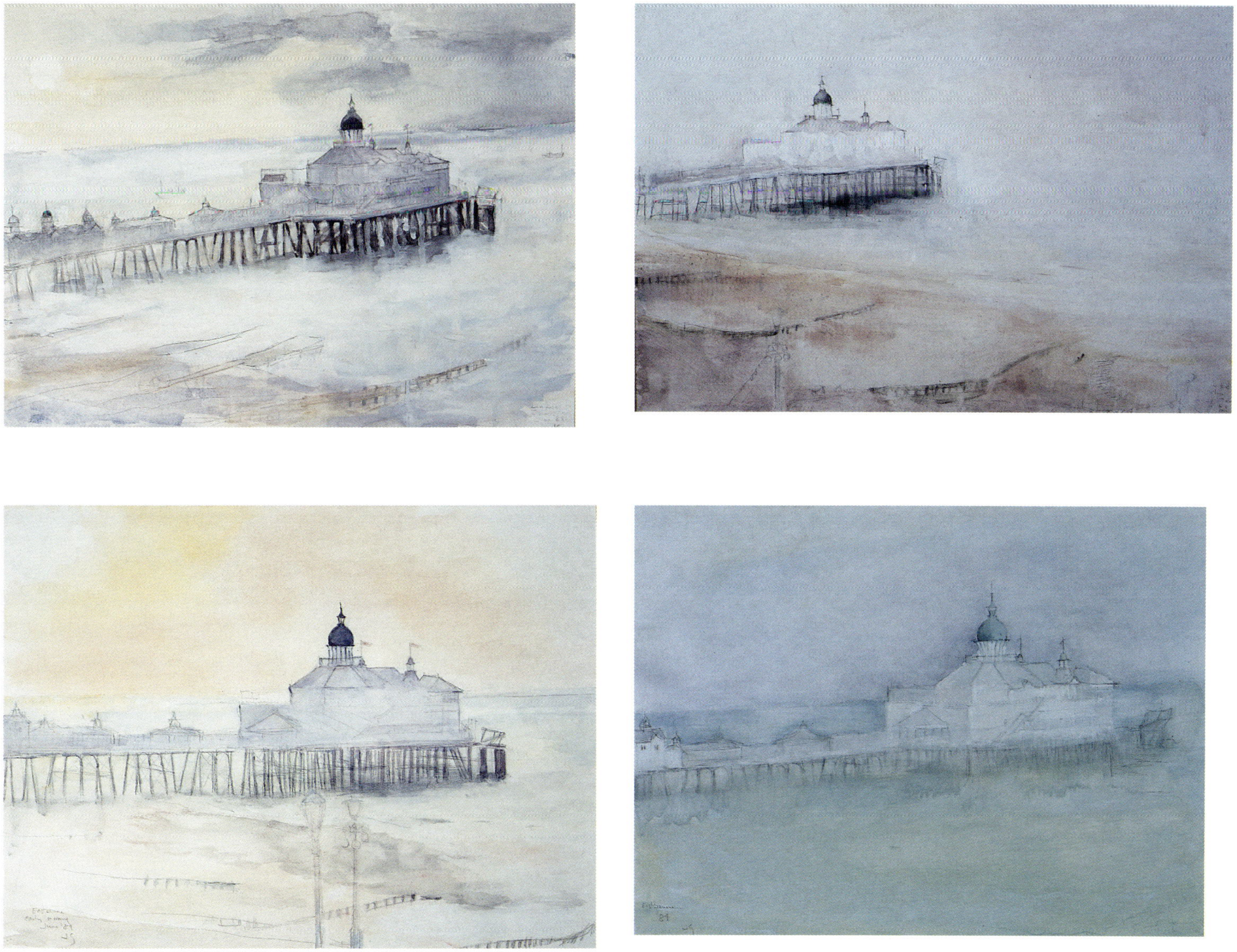

Eastbourne Pier early morning.

wonderful view of the pier. Over the years we often had different rooms on different floors, so that I had slightly different angles of the pier to paint. I must have done twelve or so paintings from the hotel windows, and then I did other paintings from outside. Once I remember we were in the roof with a sort of mansard window which I had to half climb out of to get a good painting view.

I often started painting at five-thirty in the morning, standing behind the bedroom curtains, with my palette and brushes and dangerously balanced water bottle. It was lovely at sunrise in spite of roars from the bed summoning me back. I painted the pier in the mornings, and in the afternoons; I painted it from our bedroom windows, and from the bandstand. I painted it from the seafront, and once I did a painting standing on the pier and looking back to the town, to an extraordinary building, the Albion Hotel, built in 1877 by the Victorian architect Sir Ernest George, formerly all red brick, with a tower, now painted white. That was an interesting experience, for while engrossed in the act of painting, and after years of having worked outside, I did not notice people watching, until this particular day when my attention was rudely caught by the most foul language. Looking up, I realised I was surrounded by a group of very rough youths. Luckily their violence was only verbal. I had become used, over the years, to my husband's extremely colourful vocabulary when he got very cross when playing some game badly, and it always made me laugh to hear his curious mixture of images put together so incongruously. So these youths, finding me completely unshockable, walked away and, head-butting each other, turned to me and said, in a very polite tone, 'Good luck with the painting'.

The food in our hotel left much to be desired, but we did not bother about this. After dinner, we'd wander into the town, where we had found a large sweet-shop, its windows ablaze with incredibly bright pink and yellow sweets, sticks of rock, sugared mice and wonderful bars of pink and white coconut ice. What an amusing painting I could have done had I thought of it then. The sticks of coconut ice were our favourite, and with a bar each we would wander along the front watching the sea and the pier lights coming on, which I meant to paint like that, all lit up – a scene I later found on a postcard of a painting by Charles Conder, *Eastbourne Pier in the Evening Light*, now in Aberdeen Art Gallery.

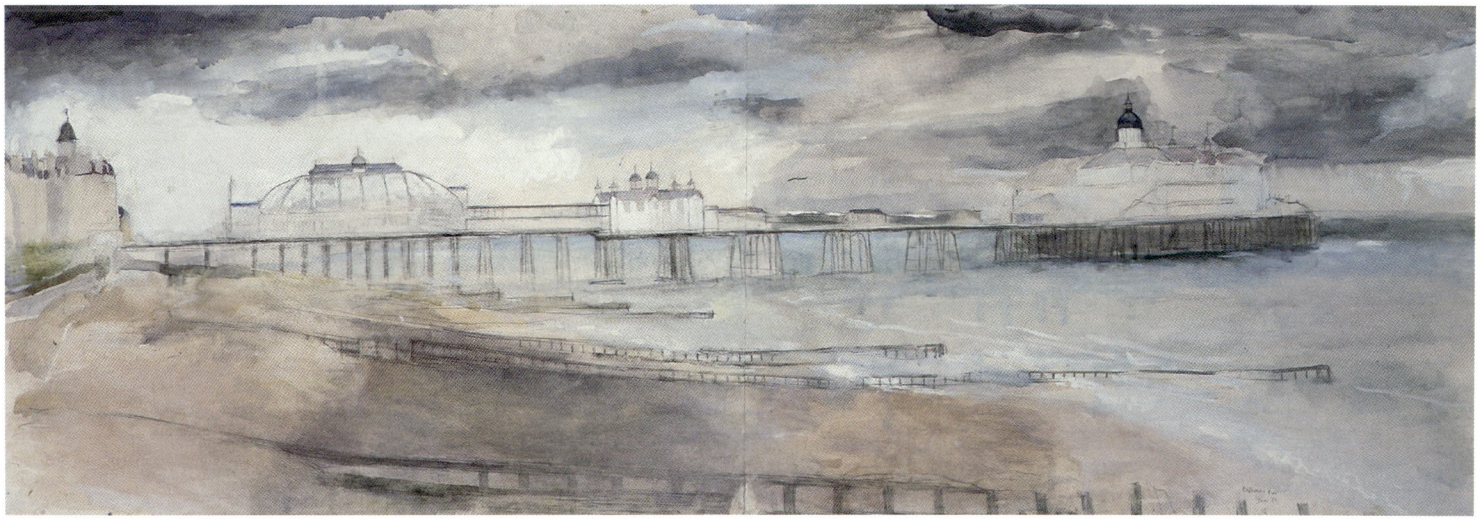

Eastbourne Pier painted from bandstand.

The croquet club was at Compton, outside the town, and the polite croquet players rarely ventured down to the front and real 'seaside'. One evening, as we meandered along each eating a large bar of coconut ice, we were greeted by Richard Rothwell, the elegant and rather Edwardian secretary of the Croquet Association based at the fashionable Hurlingham Club, famed for croquet and polo. Richard was dressed immaculately in dark blue blazer, white flannel trousers and Panama hat. He seemed quite unfazed by our informality.

In those days we went to croquet tournaments held at Cheltenham (where I painted a lot), we also went to Hurlingham, Roehampton and to Wrest Park, but mostly, and as far as this book is concerned, we spent our croquet weeks at Eastbourne, Budleigh Salterton, Southwick Park near Brighton, and at Hunstanton in Norfolk.

HOVE AND BRIGHTON HOUSES, BUDLEIGH SALTERTON, SIDMOUTH AND HUNSTANTON

Southwick Park is further west along the coast from Brighton, so for the croquet tournaments we compromised and stayed in Hove, unfortunately in a back street so that I had to walk to my 'subject'. I did a little watercolour of a square in Hove on a stormy day, and then I climbed down on to the beach and painted Brighton looking up to the big houses on the front towards Kemp Town. I included this in my exhibition at the Royal West of England Academy in Bristol in 1988, and the Academy's council bought that painting for its permanent collection. When I was painting it, with my battered old sketching easel stuck into the beach, I looked up and noticed someone watching me from behind the emerald green railings that so decoratively bordered the esplanade at Brighton. He was an odd-looking man. The next day, as I painted from the same spot, I saw him again looking at me. Towards the end of the day I watched anxiously as he climbed down towards me. 'Are you a man or a woman?' he asked. I was wearing trousers and an old fishing hat. He looked wild-eyed and smelled of drink. We were quite alone, with not another soul in sight, so I packed up as quickly as possible and scuttled off, and didn't go back to that spot.

Instead, the next day I started a painting of two large houses high on the front, one room thick, with windows on both sides, so that the threateningly stormy sky showed right through, black and forbidding. It was an intriguing subject, but before I could finish it the heavens opened and I was drenched, saving my painting only by holding it under my sweater and going on with it in the shelter of our hotel room. I did not paint the pier on that visit, but decided to return in the future. I didn't know it would be some eight years before I would go back, that in the meantime my dearest husband would die, and that I would have a terrible accident, which landed me in hospital for three months, and suffer months of disability leaving me unable to do anything for nearly a year.

I did subsequently go back and paint both of Brighton's great piers, and I will write about them later. In the meantime, I still had my husband to accompany to croquet tournaments, and we went several times to Budleigh Salterton in Devon. I painted it, and painted it, and found it a delight: so much to paint, no pier but so much else, and so many stories to tell of it.

We would stay at the Rosemullion Hotel, a long Edwardian building, gabled at each end, and built half-way up the cliff facing the sea,

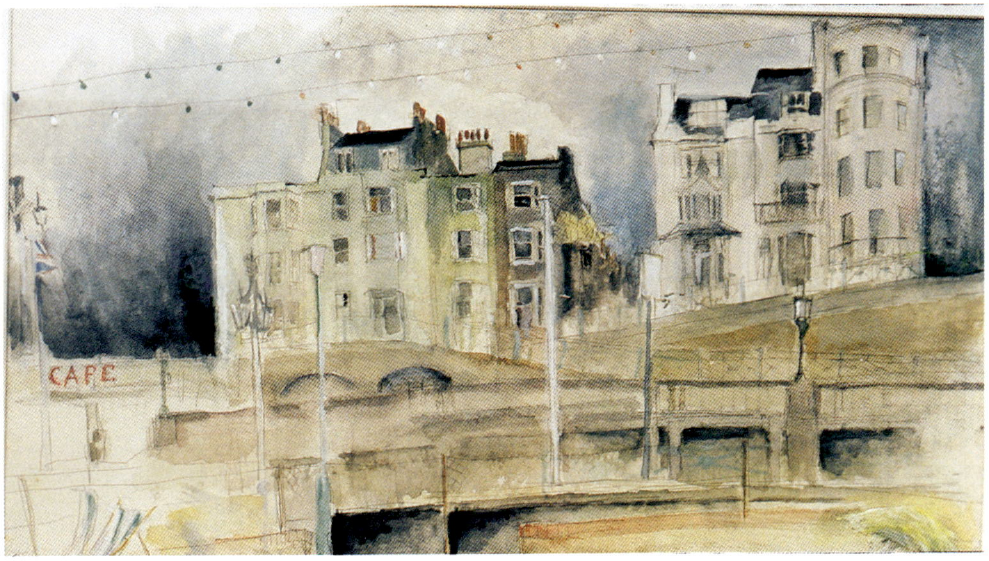

Brighton houses painted from beach, very stormy day.

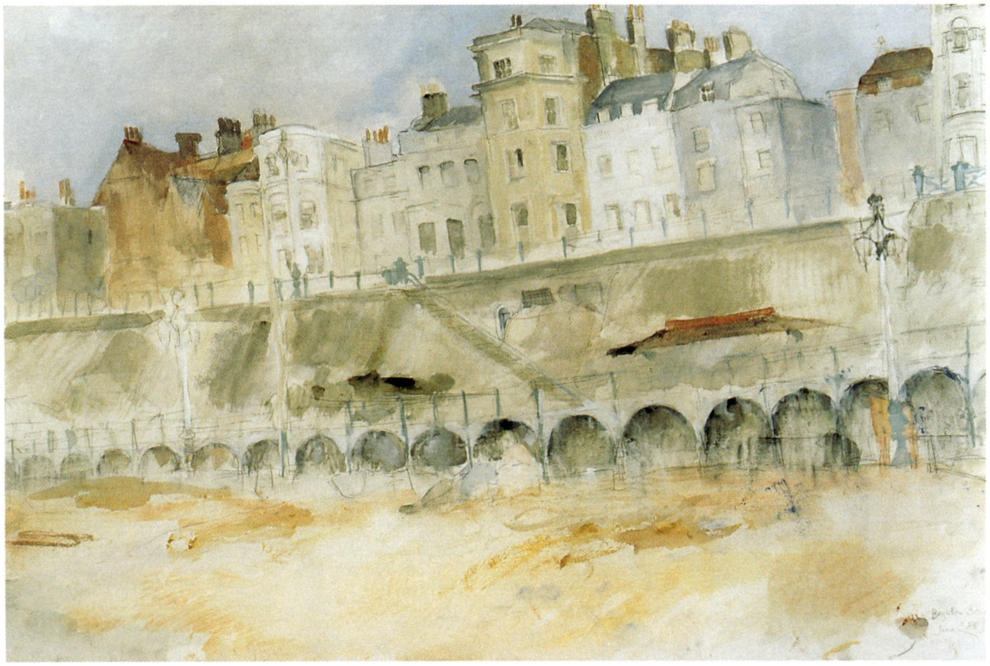

Brighton houses. [RWA Permanent Collection]

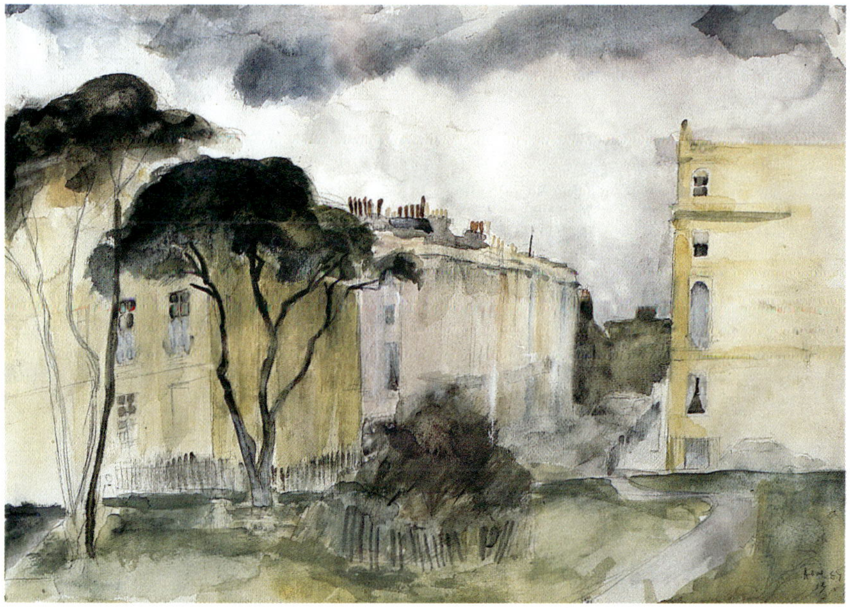

Brighton: square in nearby Hove, very stormy day.

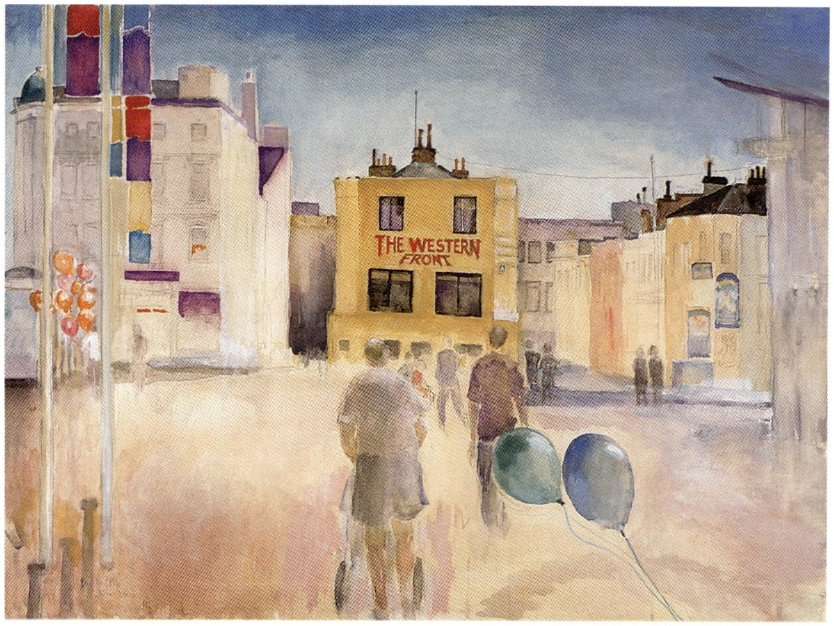

Brighton: new shopping centre
and public house.

the curve of the bay lying below it. On our first visit we had the end bedroom, on the land side. The main windows faced the sea, but as we entered I saw that from a side window the room had an intriguing view of an extraordinary house that truly caught my imagination. Its roof was on a level with my window some twenty feet away, there were four or five gables of different sizes in odd juxtaposition to each other, five chimney stacks, one with a window in it, odd-shaped chimney pots of varying heights, one very tall indeed. The roofs were of slate and the house was white painted stucco. Between the many separate roofs were small flat grey areas with the odd dormer window and little doors opening on to them. It was like a fantasy by Mervyn Peake. A large house, with the rooms, I imagined, on many different levels, and my extraordinary view of it, looking down across to the roof, gave it an even more unreal appearance. I cannot ever remember looking at it from the road that ran in front, or from any other angle, almost as if this surreal picture was enough, with all its details filled in by my imagination. Its address, The Cliffe, Cliff Road, gave nothing away, nothing at all of its haunted strangeness.

I started painting this strange house the next morning. We were to be there for a week and one evening, as I watched out of that side window for my husband's return from his match, the light beginning to fade into blue, a few street lights coming on, another painting resolved itself: a painting that had to be got down very quickly, that disappeared as I looked at it, that by working the same time each day I managed to capture, making its magic my own, a painting that I still love and wander in and will not part with. I captured it then, but I never got the chance to do so again. We stayed at the Rosemullion Hotel many more times over the years, but we never entered that room again. Its door was always locked, and no one would tell me why.

In subsequent years when I wanted to paint The Cliffe I had to climb up a fire-escape, further along on the side wall of the hotel and paint from there. The last time I did so was in 1988, the last time we were to stay in Budleigh Salterton. I will never forget how cold I got climbing on to that rusty iron stair-rail, so cold I could hardly climb down when I had finished painting.

In May, 1989 our letter to the Rosemullion to reserve a room went unanswered, and on going down to investigate we found a great hole in the ground . . . no hotel, no garden, no long-term residents, only a board advertising that a block of flats was to be erected on that beautiful site.

Sometimes after a morning spent painting, I would set out to explore the little town and once discovered a strange and charming little thatched building, set back from a long green lawn and facing the sea. Fairlynch was the Budleigh Salterton Arts Centre and Museum. Its glass cases were filled with rocks, pebbles, maps, a geological survey of the area, and books on its history, how it had once been an important port, until in the sixteenth century a great storm had, over one terrible night, silted the whole bay with stones, the harbour disappearing completely.

The little museum was open only at certain times on certain days, and one afternoon, taking time off from painting, I went there to browse, and found a book on the history of some of its erstwhile residents. To my joy I found a memoir on Thomas Nadauld Brushfield, born in December 1828, in Church Street, Spitalfields. Dr Brushfield had built and lived in The Cliffe – my painting subject, my current obsession. I sat down, enthralled, to read.

Dr Brushfield had trained at the London Hospital, starting there in 1845 and in 1851 went to Chester Asylum as a house surgeon, becoming in 1854 the Medical Superintendent, taking on with great keenness the most splendid work of his life. In those days the role of Medical Superintendent was all important; indeed, we had inside knowledge of that as in 1950 the superintendent of our local mental hospital, a hospital of some two thousand patients, was a close friend. He was rather like the ruler of a small kingdom in his huge Victorian house fully staffed by his high grade patients in the middle of the hospital grounds. He would from time to time throw splendid parties, and the champagne, presented by the families of some of his rich private patients, literally flowed.

But Dr Brushfield was an idealist, and he set out to institute reforms in these huge institutions, devoting the rest of his working life to improving life for his patients. One of his first moves was to dispense with every form of mechanical restraint – the straight-jacket was at once abolished – and his staff were made to understand that no violence was to be used to control the patients. The only restraint, by which even the most violent patient could come to no harm, was the padded room, and that, in time, was very rarely required.

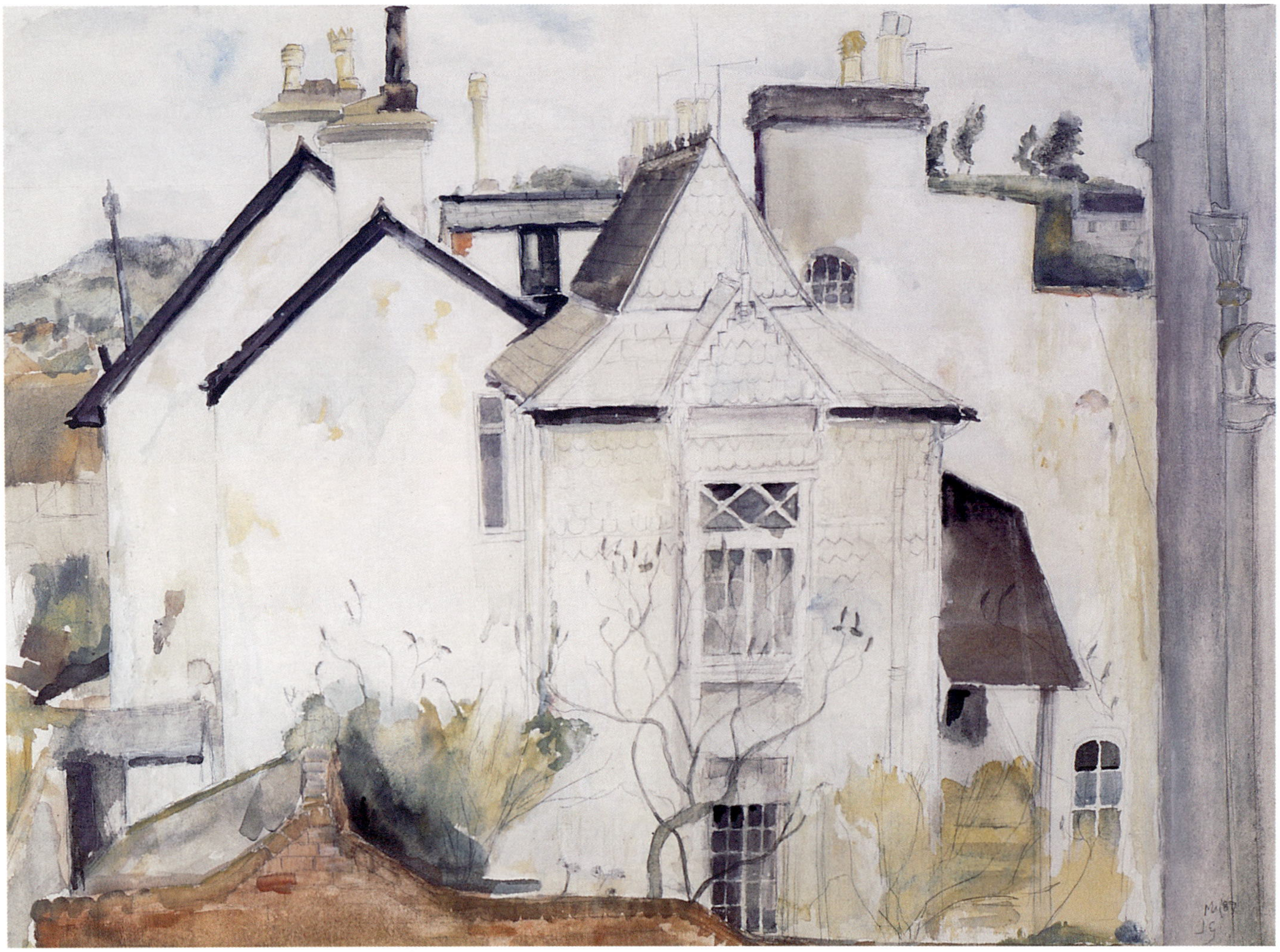

Budleigh Salterton: The Cliffe, built by Dr. Thomas Brushfield.

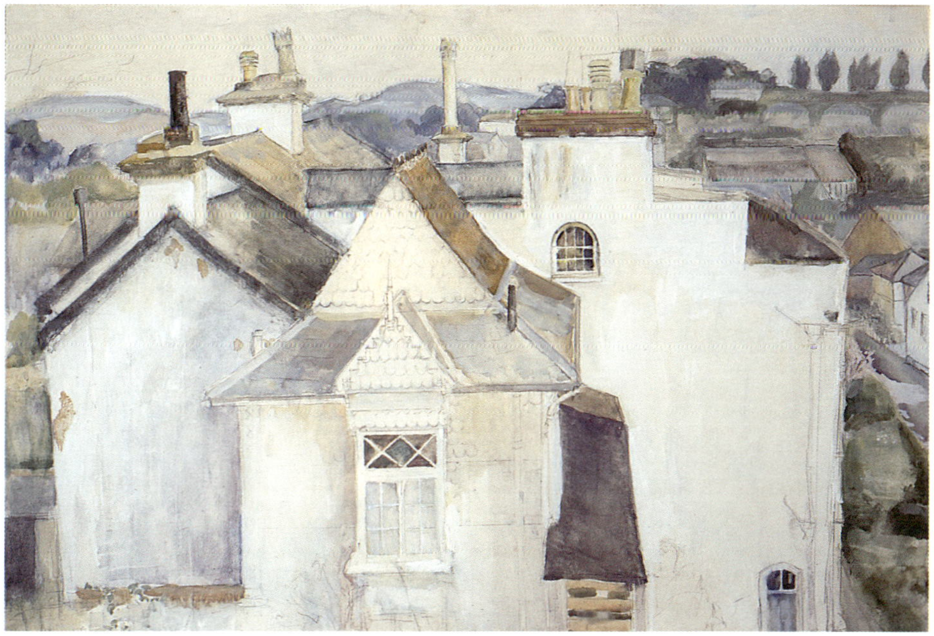

The Cliffe.

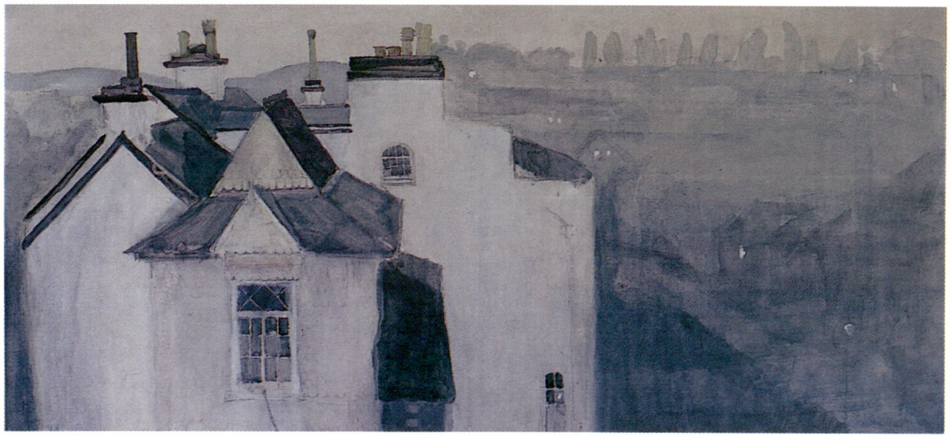

In evening light.

In 1866 he had taken his MD at St Andrews University and had then been invited to take over as Medical Superintendent at the newly built asylum at Brookwood in Surrey. The new job was exciting as he would have a hand in designing the buildings and could carry out his ideas of non-restraint. Early in his time there, he built a large recreational hall, with a stage, and indeed everything needed for the giving of concerts, plays, dances and entertainments of all sorts. There were something like 2,000 patients and 200 attendants and servants, and also a garden and farm. For 16 years, Dr Brushfield was a benevolent autocrat, able to carry out his enlightened ideas for the treatment of the insane.

Sadly, all this came to a tragic end. One of his patients hid behind a partly opened door, through which the Doctor was due to enter on his rounds, and with a heavy earthenware vessel struck him on the head, giving him a serious scalp wound and knocking him unconscious. It was many months before Dr Brushfield could leave his bed, and after a long convalescence he reluctantly decided he should retire. In 1882 he came to Budleigh Salterton and built his house – my house, The Cliffe – and living there for the next thirty years, researched and wrote a life of Sir Walter Raleigh. Raleigh had been born in the village of East Budleigh, a mile or so from Budleigh Salterton. It was a life of Raleigh, but also a vivid description of life at the time and of the vindictiveness of those in authority, culminating in the death on the scaffold of this splendid soldier and sailor early in the reign of King James I.

Living here at The Cliffe, with many unused rooms, the good doctor amassed a vast library, and he was able to give ready help to his old friend, Dr J.H. Murray in Oxford in preparing his magnum opus, *A New English Dictionary on Historical Principles*, now of course known as *The Oxford English Dictionary*. Murray had assembled a team of researchers, sending in slips noting from their research the first known usage of particular words. Dr Brushfield submitted over 72,000 slips, and the extent of his reading must have been staggering. He was still working in 1908, in his eightieth year and there, sadly, I lost track of him. But The Cliffe is his memorial, that strange and haunted house that I so loved to look at and to paint; and now I had found its history, while browsing in the museum.

At the bottom of Budleigh High Street the road opened out with the pebble beach and the sea on one side and a row of houses on the other. The first house I was interested in was a white three-storeyed hexagonal building facing the sea, on its front a blue circular plaque recording that Sir John Millais had rented the house from Lady Rolle of Bicton Park, a great country house just a few miles from Budleigh. This little house was her sea-side abode. Millais had taken the house in 1870 in order to paint *The Boyhood of Raleigh*. He had his two sons, Everett and George, pose as the young Walter Raleigh and his friend Humphrey Gilbert (the coloniser of Newfoundland), both dressed in Elizabethan costume. He then found a retired sailor to sit on the low wall – the wall is still there – and this old salt regaled them with stories of sailing and discovery, an enactment of a scene that might well have occurred some three hundred years before.

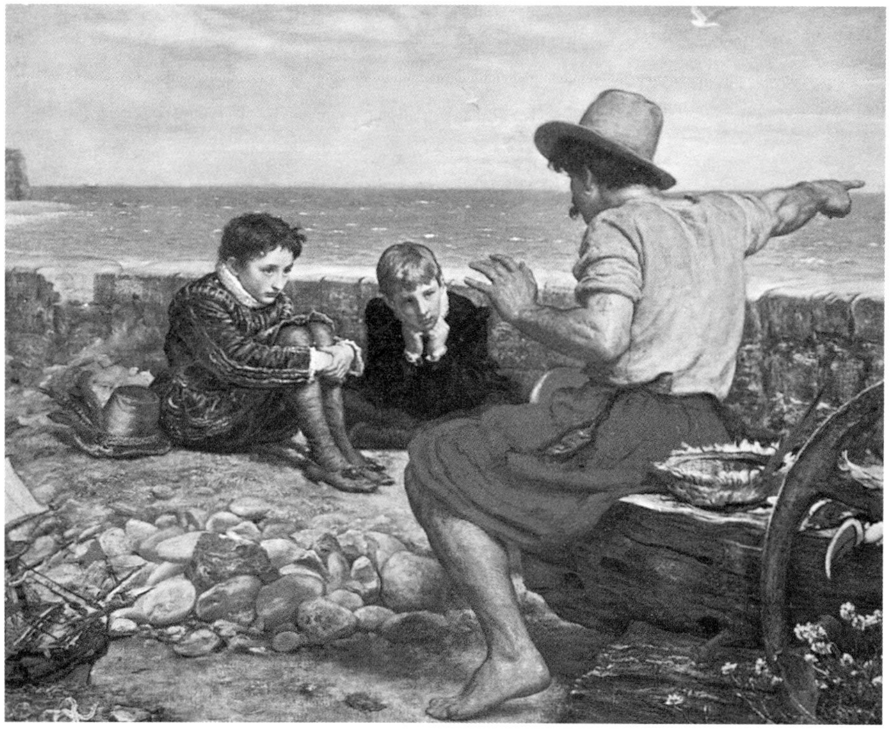

The Boyhood of Raleigh, oil, Sir John Everett Millais. [Trustees of the Tate Gallery, London]

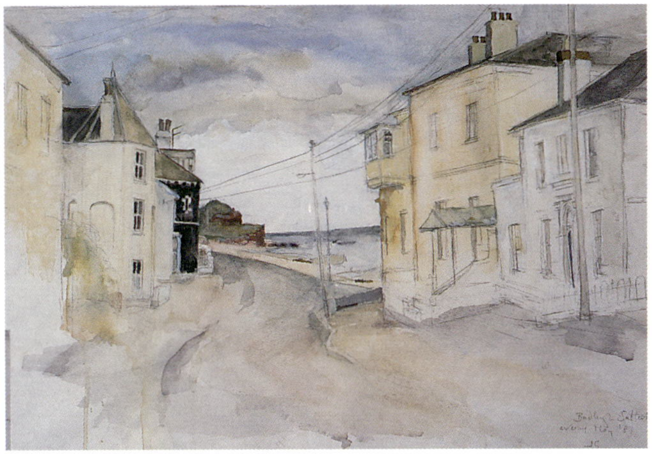

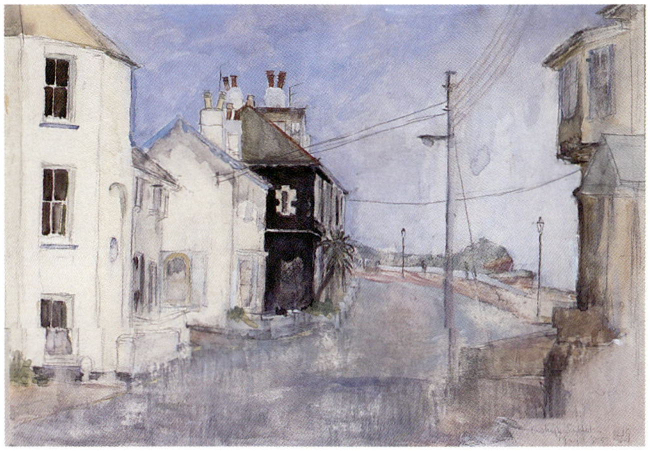

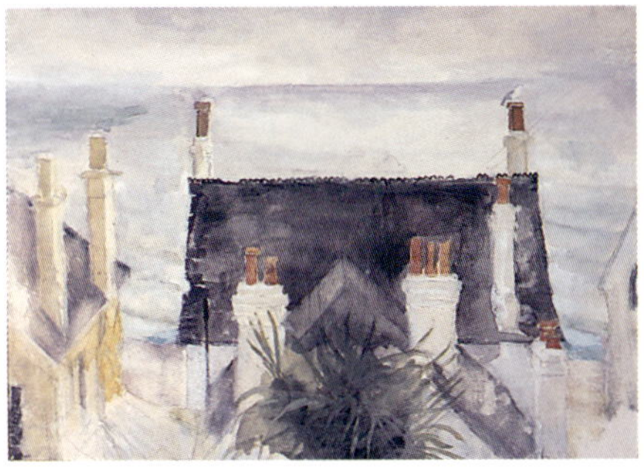

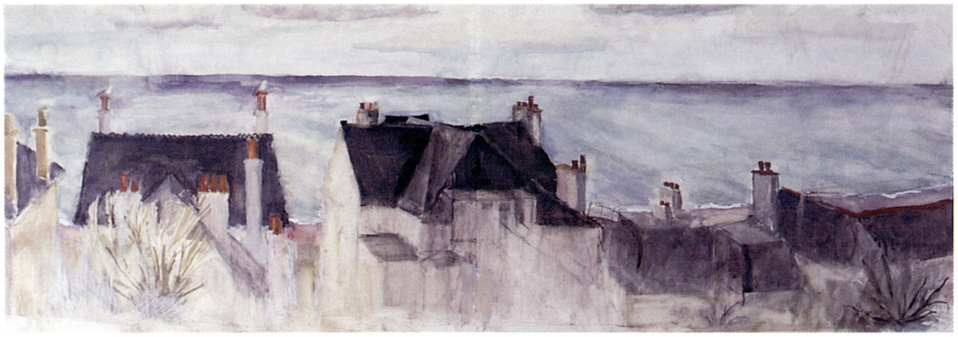

Top The beach end of Budleigh Salterton's High Street, with house that Sir John Millais stayed in while painting *The Boyhood of Raleigh*.

Bottom Budleigh Salterton houses from Madeira Drive.

sort of terrace wondered if I had broken anything, realising that I might not be found, because no-one would know where I was. I picked myself up and found a way round the deserted house and down to the front and back to the hotel, resolved to be more sensible in future.

My husband's last croquet tournament in Budleigh was in May, 1989. With the Rosemullion gone, we decided to stay a few miles away in Sidmouth. I did one painting there, sitting on the top of the stone steps going down to the beach. Looking one way, I could see the crescent of Regency houses where we were staying, and turning to look the other way I could see the low red cliffs and the fishing boats pulled up on the beach. While I was painting, my husband came back to see if I was alright, knowing I had little common sense. He took one look and said, with some concern, that I was quite blue. I was, indeed, extremely cold, almost too cold to move, but move I had to, and set off to search the little town for some sort of anorak to keep me warm – an awful waste of painting time.

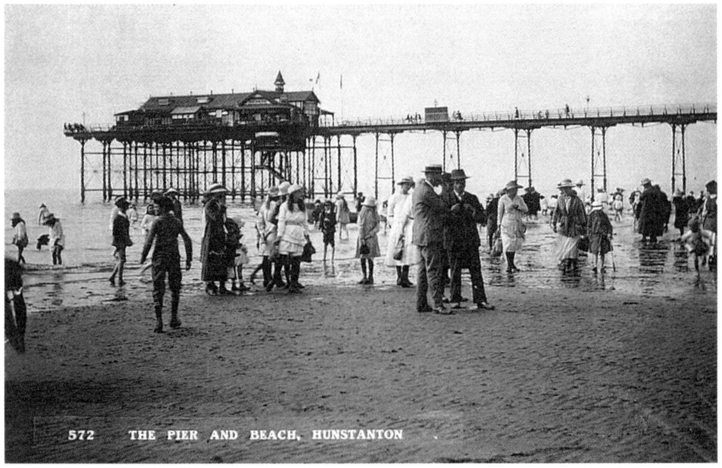

The Pier, Hunstanton.

Our days of croquet and painting together were sadly coming to an end. We had one more tournament together at Hunstanton in Norfolk. The drive there was lovely. We looked at Ely's wonderful cathedral and visited Blickling Hall, a great early brick house built in 1616, now run by the National Trust. We stopped at Kings Lynn, a delightful little town. It was one of the very few times – indeed, it turned out to be the last – that I could persuade my husband to stop and look.

When we arrived at Hunstanton, we found the hotel we had booked was a sort of family hotel set in the sand dunes. On the beach, across from the hotel, and almost buried in the dunes, was a group of beach huts. The next morning I set out to paint them, but I managed only a sketch before it started to rain. I could have done a really interesting painting there, but it was not to be. The rain was never to stop while we were there, but the little sketch, which I reproduce here in this book, drew the comment from George Sweet, who taught me to paint, 'That is a delicious little watercolour'. It hangs now outside my bedroom door to remind me of very happy days.

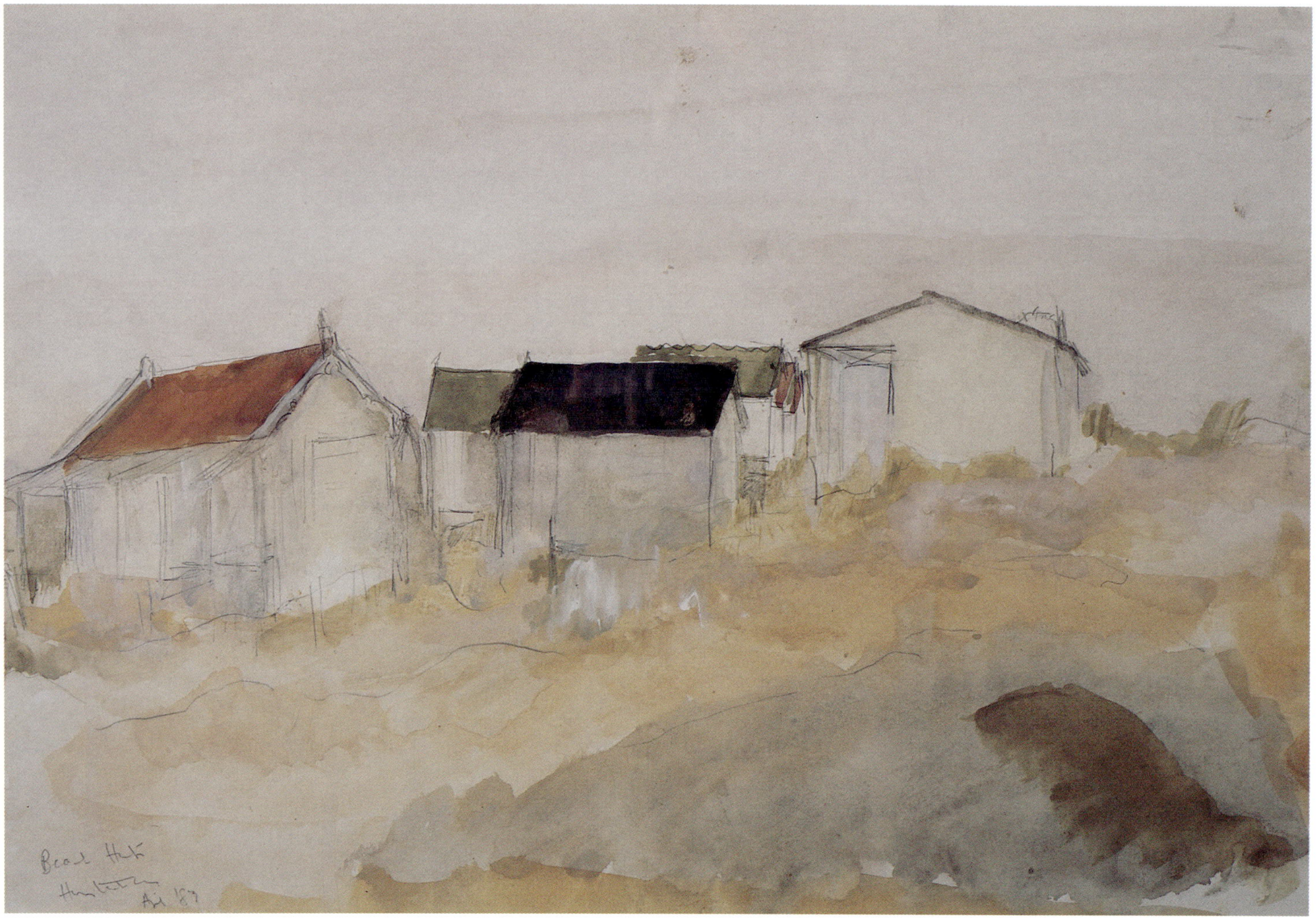

Hunstanton beach huts.

ALDEBURGH, LYME REGIS, FINDOCHTY – AND THE PALACE PIER AT BRIGHTON

My husband died in 1989 and by 1991 I had managed to pull myself together sufficiently to paint a series of watercolours of Henley. I held an exhibition of them at Phyllis Court Club in the summer of that year and it did very well. In the early spring I had stayed for a few days with my sister in Essex, from where we visited Gainsborough's House in Sudbury, the art gallery and museum in the house where the painter had been born. My sister was chairman of one of their committees. On leaving Sudbury, we spent two days at Aldeburgh and I painted a little sketch of houses on the front and the edge of the sea. It snowed, it was early April, and I froze as I painted, and eventually being picked up by my sister could hardly move. I see that I wrote on the picture, 'April, Very Cold!'

In the following four years I attended the Henley Royal Regatta on each of the five days. I would walk through 'Stewards' along the course to the start, beyond Temple Island, carrying my painting things and mingling with the smart crowd, but not of it, drawing, painting and photographing as I went. In this way, I could gather enough material to turn my sketches into finished oil paintings, working on them in the intervening winters. I had enough work for two exhibitions of 'People at the Regatta', held at the Phyllis Court Club in 1994 and 1996.

All this activity was stopped by the dreadful accident that nearly killed me. Perhaps experience – even awful experience – is given one to use, and while lying in a hospital ward unable to move, I had time to think and plan a book I had always wanted to write and that eventually became *Spey Portrait*.

By 1997 I was ready to start thinking about going away to paint again, and to do what I had long wanted to do: continue with the series of paintings of piers, of the sea, and of seaside houses that I had started when my husband was still alive. I am now not allowed to drive, and a friend had to accompany me; in fact, two good friends came alternately. I tried to go in May and again in September, for a week at a time, feeling rather like Turner illustrating the Ports of England. The illustrations in this book are the result of these expeditions: the early ones done while accompanying my husband on his croquet journeys, the later ones, done after his death, giving me a reason to go away, to go to the sea, which I love and feel so far from, living here in the middle of England.

The first place we visited was Lyme Regis, and though I had always wanted to go there I didn't immediately 'see' a painting. I did the little sketch looking down the main street to the sea that I reproduce here. Still rather doddery, I looked at the Cobb and did a drawing, but I did not find it easy to start painting again. I think we went to Lyme twice, rather more for my convalescence than for serious painting.

In the autumn of 1997, I really got going and we stayed at the Royal Albion Hotel in Brighton, built in 1826, the hotel that years before I had imagined would have a grand view of the Palace Pier. The company set up to build the Palace was formed in 1886 and it was to be built to replace the great chain pier. Work started in 1891, but the company ran into financial difficulties, and the pier was not finished until the philanthropist Sir John Howard stepped in. The pier finally opened on May 20th, 1899. Its design, by R. St George Moore, is the most Oriental of all in design, not surprising perhaps, as it stands almost opposite John Nash's Royal Pavilion. Originally, it was entered through three lacy segmental arches surmounted by cresting and illuminated. These illuminations were repeated all the way down the length of the pier, but in 1930 the entrance was replaced by a more conventional jubilee-type clock tower when the promenade was set back for road widening.

Where the pier widens there is a series of kiosks, all very Oriental in design, and the balustrades and all the iron-work are of most delicate scroll patterns. Over the years, many additions have been made but nearly all in matching style, and it was always intended that the pier should have a concert hall or pavilion at its sea end. This was not begun until the pier was opened and completed in 1901. I have not been able to establish when the helter-skelter was built, but it always features in my paintings, and I am glad of its colour, and its stripes. This really is a 'fun' pier.

At the same time, another concert hall (now the Palace of Fun) was built halfway down the pier. The Palace is now listed Grade II*. Somewhere, I think, Somerset Maugham said that every composition should have a beginning, a midde and an end, and Brighton thus fulfils this criterion as far as piers are concerned, for the chain pier was the beginning, the West Pier the middle and the Palace Pier virtually the

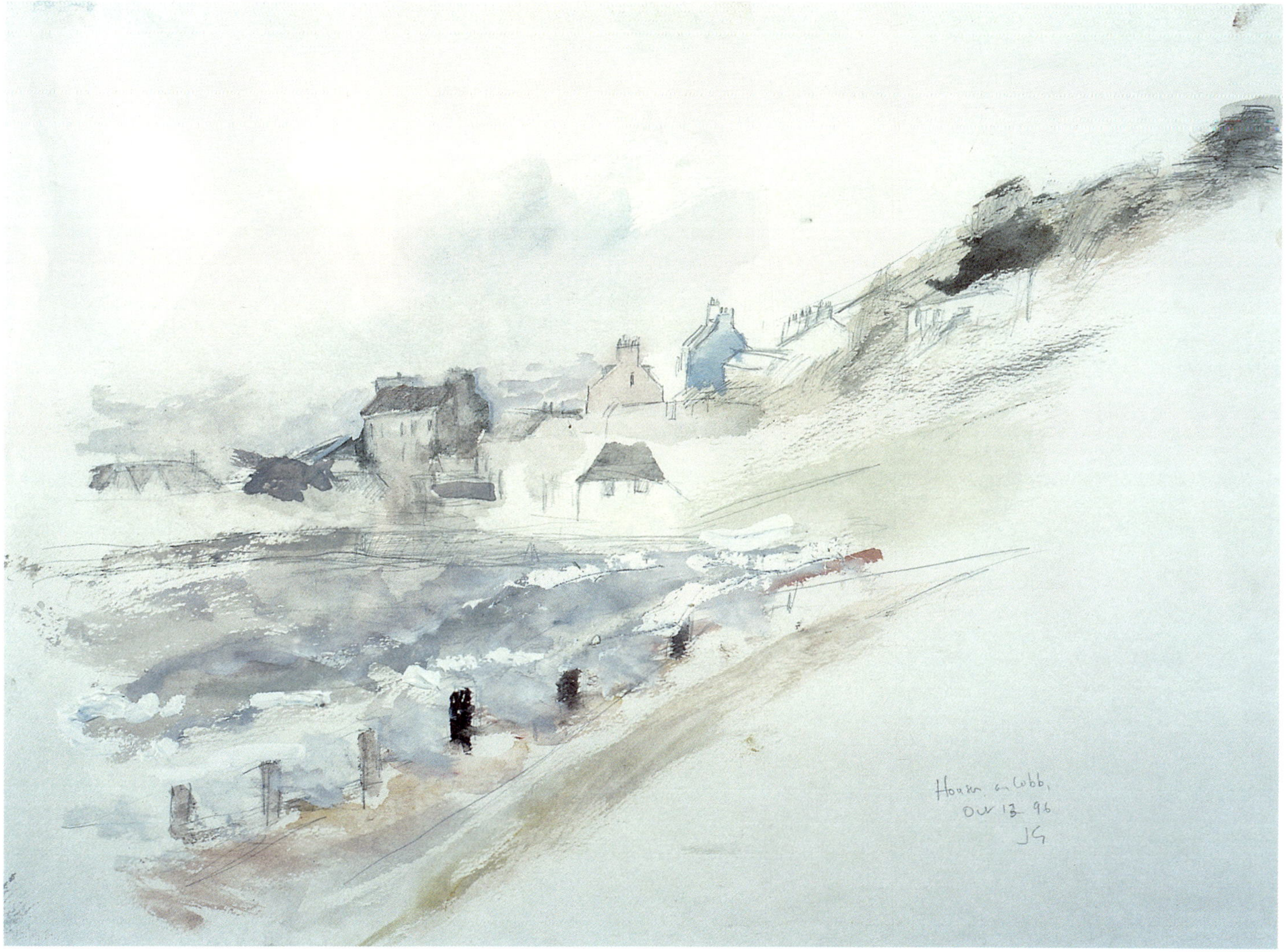

Lyme Regis: houses near The Cobb.

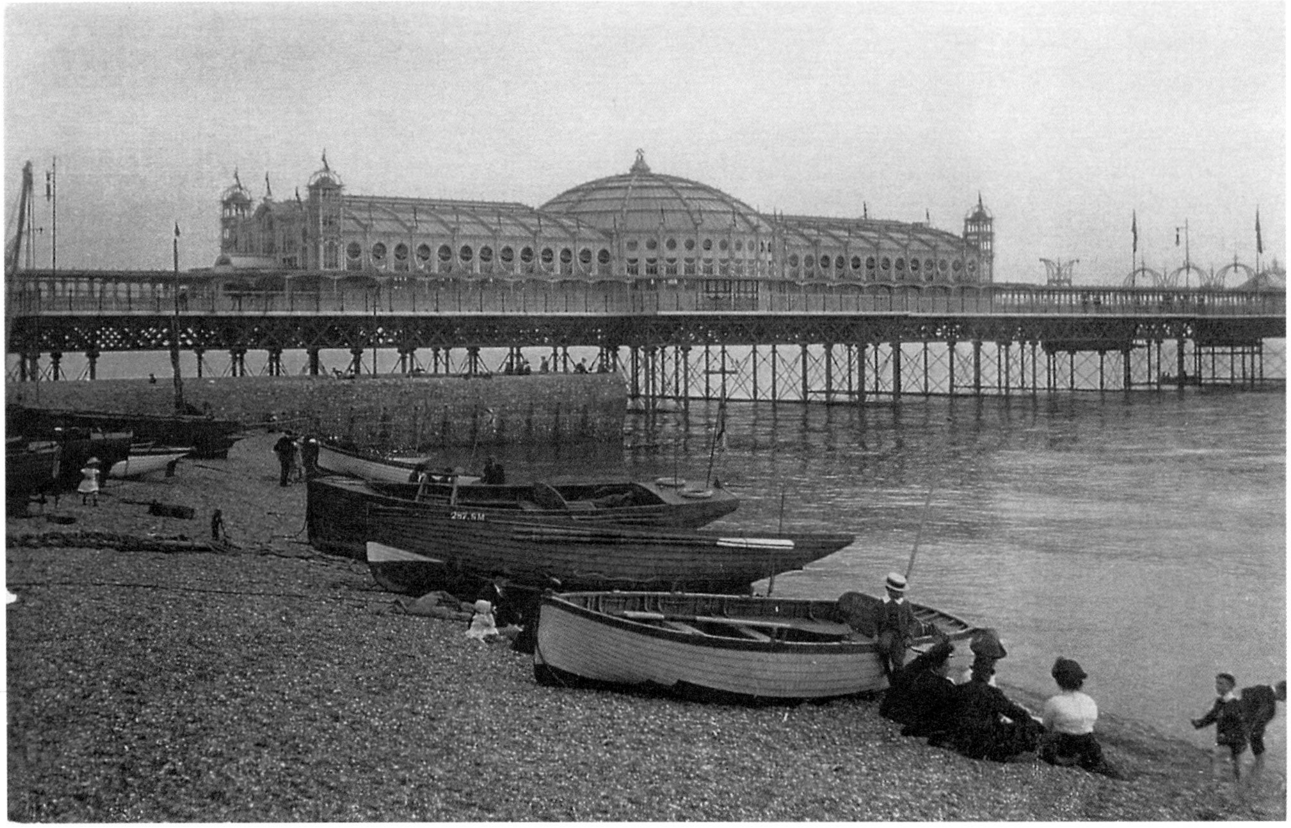

Winter Gardens, Brighton's Palace Pier, 1913.

end. Very few piers were built after 1900. Brighton Palace Pier is thirty years younger than the once very beautiful West Pier. It is probably the best of the surviving piers, and if it is true that cast iron will not stand in the sea for longer than 100 years, then something must be done to preserve it now.

My idea to stay at The Royal Albion was a good one, for the hotel was perfectly situated, the bedroom large and light. I stood fixed at the windows for there, lying before me, was exactly the picture I wanted. For the next week I scarcely moved, just walking for an hour in the afternoons. We walked up to 99 Marine Parade, where I had been stationed as a Torpedo Wren in 1943, only to find that the tall yellow house where we lived had completely disappeared, but the Royal Crescent, where we had our lectures on torpedoes, depth charges, gun firing circuits and ships' telephones – all of which we were taught to service – was still intact and now listed. It was built in 1798-1807, the earliest unified composition in Brighton, a crescent following those at Bath and Buxton.

LLANDUDNO, BANGOR – AND BRIGHTON AGAIN

In May, 1998 we went to Llandudno in north Wales, primarily for me to paint another pier. We had the most lovely drive through Bala and picnicked by a small bubbling river flowing into the lake. The primroses were out, the lambs leaping. The sun shone, all heaven seemed to be around.

We reached Llandudno. Sadly, we didn't have a view of the pier from our hotel windows, but we could see the beginning of the entrance to the pier, and the huge Grand Hotel, once indeed a fine building, but now a Butlin's holiday camp. One morning I awoke very early, and drawing back the curtains 'saw' a picture, and started painting straightaway; it was misty, insubstantial, interesting. So I was able to do one painting, at least, from the bedroom window.

To paint the pier I had to be driven round the Great Orme, a large rocky headland. The pier looked particularly good in the afternoon light from there, quite white against the deep ultramarine blue of the sea. Of the piers not designed by Eugenius Birch, the first of any significance was Llandudno. It is listed as a Grade II* building; dating from 1876, it is the work of Brunlees and McKerrow. It has had a pavilion added at its sea end but, apart from this, it still presents very much the appearance of one of the early piers sustaining nothing but a series of very elegant, largish octagonal kiosks with wide overhanging eaves. The pier is unusual in that it does not, as most piers do, follow a single straight line, but takes a turn of nearly 45 degrees about a third of the way down its length. I stood at the top of some steep steps leading down to the rocks and the sea. The pier lay on my right, I propped myself up against a rock and just managed to fit in my old sketching easel. I put up two pages from my watercolour sketch book, pinned onto a board with the large paperclips that I always use to keep bits of paper together and to fix them to various lengths of hardboard as, for some reason, I never seem to have with me paper big enough or long enough for my particular picture.

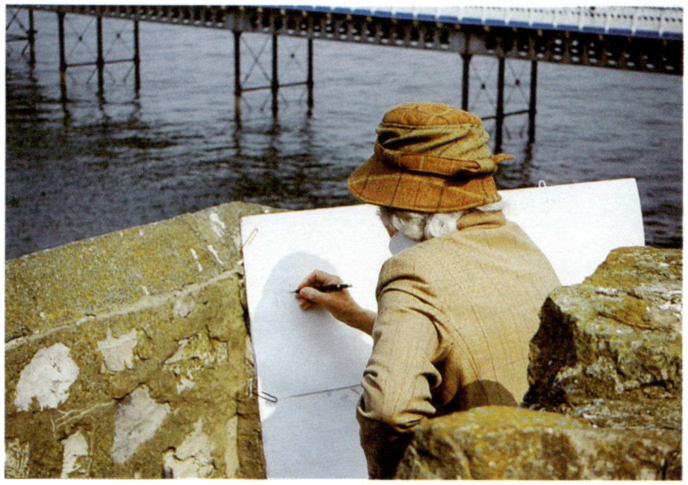

The author drawing the pier at Llandudno. [photo: Angela Searle]

I have since found that, in this dilemma, I am not in bad company, for in the lovely little exhibition held some years ago of the Queen's Canalettos at Buckingham Palace, several of the drawings were done on two sheets of paper joined together. Leonard McComb, a very good contemporary painter, often uses large sheets of hot press paper, perhaps ten sheets or so, put together to paint or

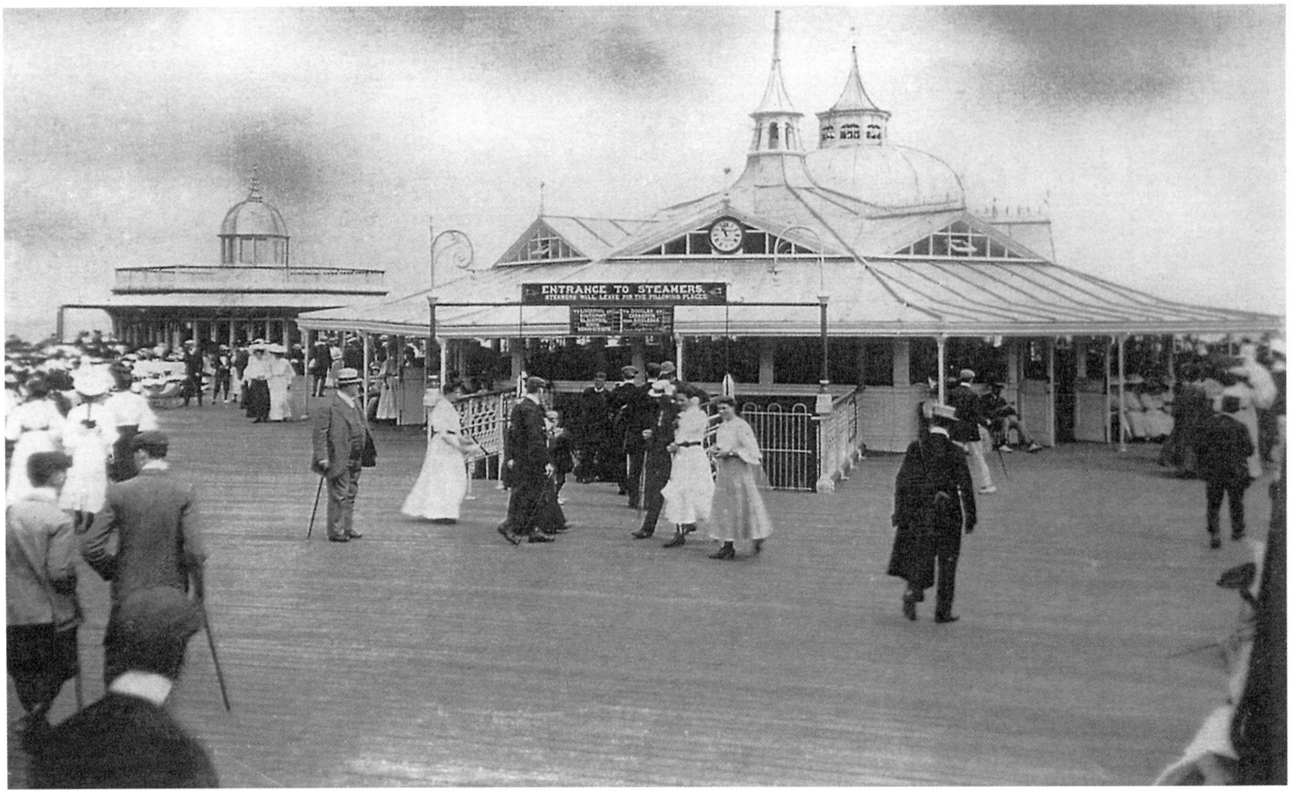

Morning promenade on the Pier Head, Llandudno, 1913.

draw on, mostly for large portraits or landscapes. I treasure the lovely letter than he sent me about the book I wrote on my dear painting master, George Sweet.

From Llandudno we drove over to Anglesey. I had always wanted to go to Plas Newydd, the Marquis of Anglesey's house, where Rex Whistler had painted a big classical wall painting which I had long wanted to see. I was not disappointed. It was such fun, so fresh, and looked as if it had just been painted: the best thing I have ever seen of Rex Whistler's – a pastiche, with echoes of Claude, Poussin, several classical painters, but done with such enthusiasm, such bravura, the whole composition flowing along beautifully. It is a real pleasure to look at and to roam in.

On our way back we stopped at the pretty little Bangor pier but there was not time to paint it and I took an inadequate photograph, just as a reminder. It was designed in 1896 by J.J. Webster and has never had any pavilions or other buildings added to it. It gives the best idea of what most of the early piers looked like when they were purely promenade-places above the sea. It has a series of very elegant polygonal kiosks with steeply curving roofs with a slight suggestion of Chinese influence about them.

In September 1998, the charming girl who had come as my nurse when I left hospital accompanied me to Brighton. I wanted to go back to paint Birch's great West Pier, the only Grade I pier in the country. On reading it up, I see that in 1866, on Saturday October 6th, 'a terrible visitation, a long and enduringly persistent sea-side drizzle' had threatened to envelope Brighton. But somehow the drizzle held off and the thousands who had gathered on the sea-front for the ceremony and celebrations marking the opening of Brighton's new pier managed to stay dry. By early afternoon 'the balconies of the houses were crowded with well dressed ladies, the King's Road was lined with equipages and pedestrians, and the shore thronged with people'. The new pier was packed with invited guests, while all other visitors had to pay an admission fee of one shilling. The pier was decorated with flags from all nations and on the pier itself music was provided by the band of the 68th Light Infantry Regiment from Portsmouth.

At two o'clock Mr Henry Moore, the chairman of the West Pier Company, declared the pier open and the Mayor of Brighton gave a speech on behalf of the townsfolk. The Royal standard was hoisted up the flag-staff on the pier-head and a gun detachment of the Coast Guard saluted it with 21 guns, fired from a couple of nine-pounders in the centre of the pier. At four o'clock, there was an inaugural dinner, attended by 140 dignitaries in the banqueting hall of the Royal Pavilion. That night the pier was illuminated and there was a grand display of fireworks.

A wonderful send-off in 1866 and now here I was, 132 years later, looking at the sad wreck of that great pier, cut off from the shore, with just a temporary walk-way to the land and the gate locked to the general public. In spite of all the damage and the battering by man and by the elements, the West Pier still had immense dignity, like some grand old dowager whose wig has slipped slightly. For me the pier, in its present state, was immensely paintable, and had so many moods and so many colours. I saw hours of pleasure lying ahead, while I would try to recapture some of its magic.

We stayed at the Metropole Hotel, built in 1888 by Waterhouse, in red brick and terracotta, five storeys and dormers: a very large, imposing

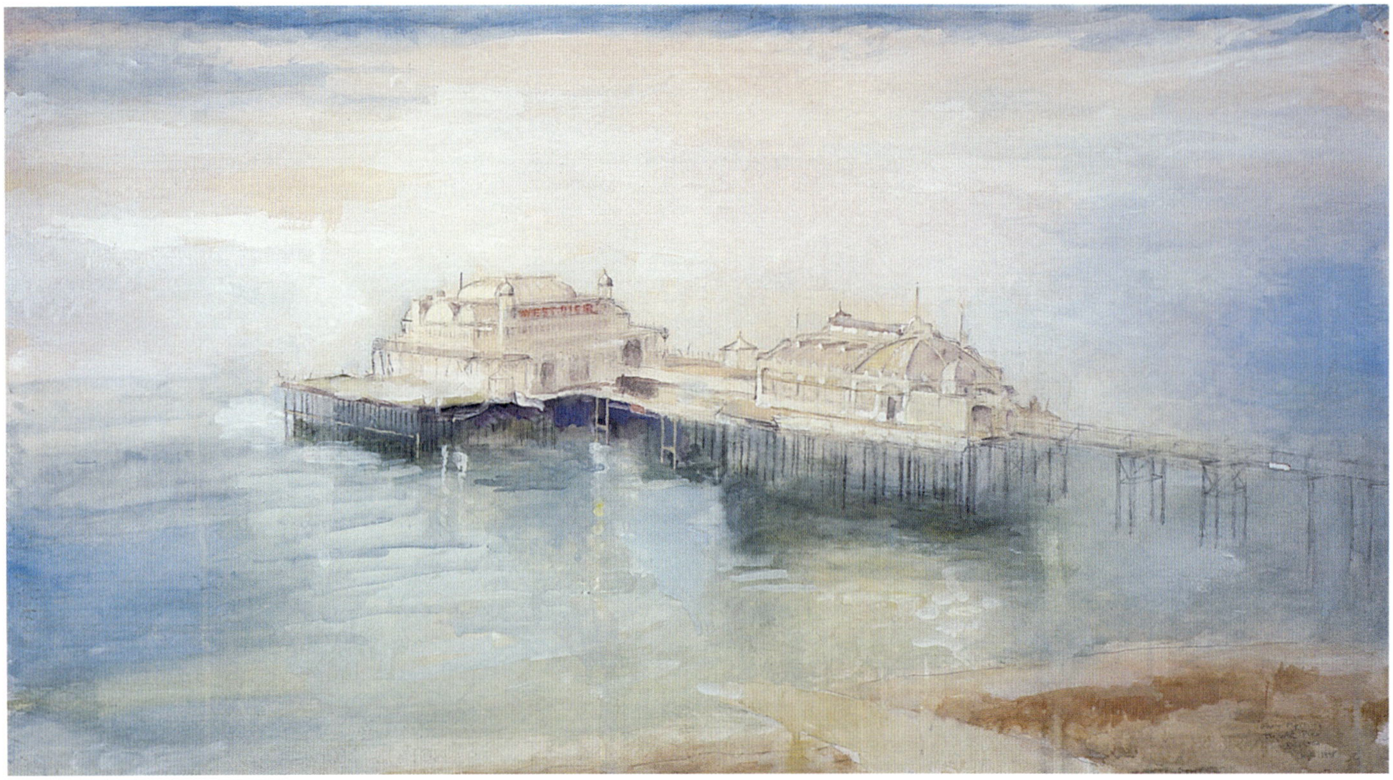

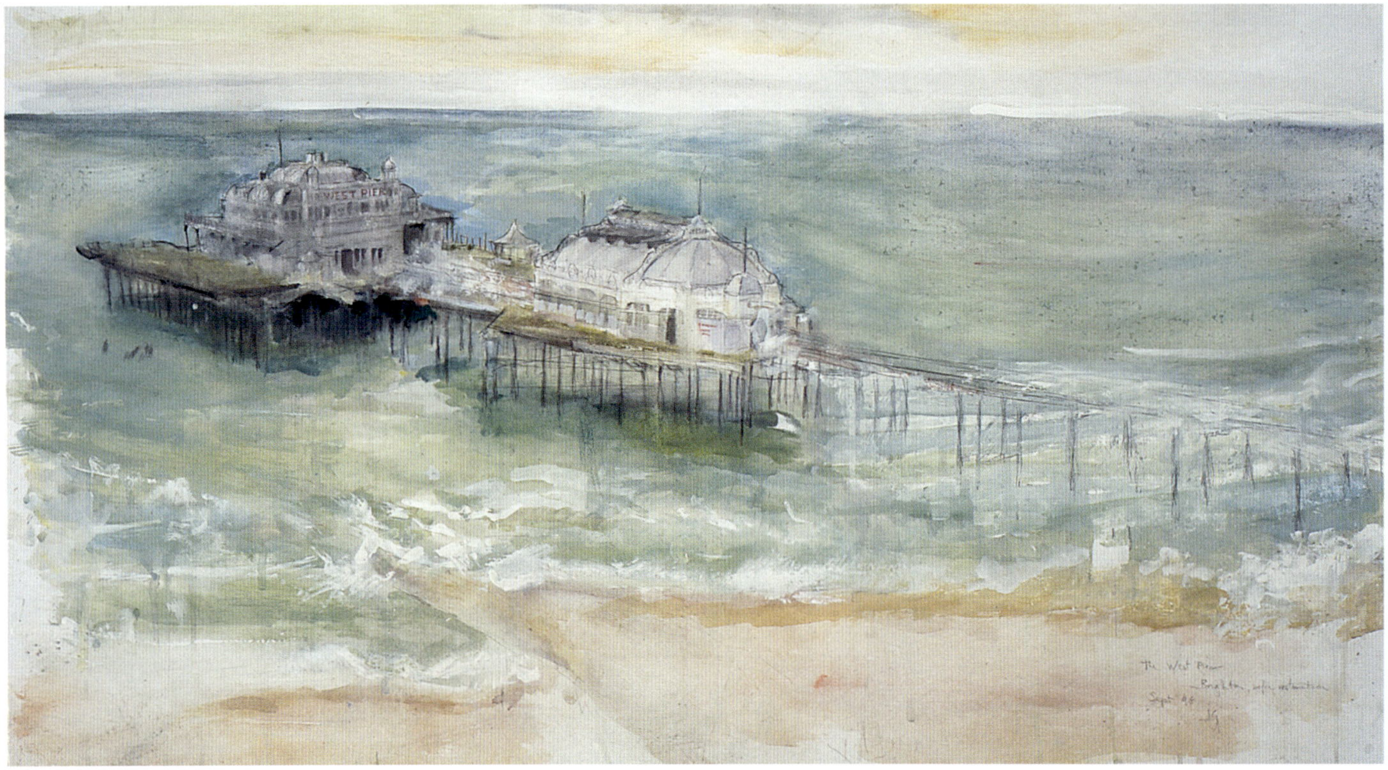

Top Brighton: The West Pier at dawn. *Bottom* In rough seas, early afternoon

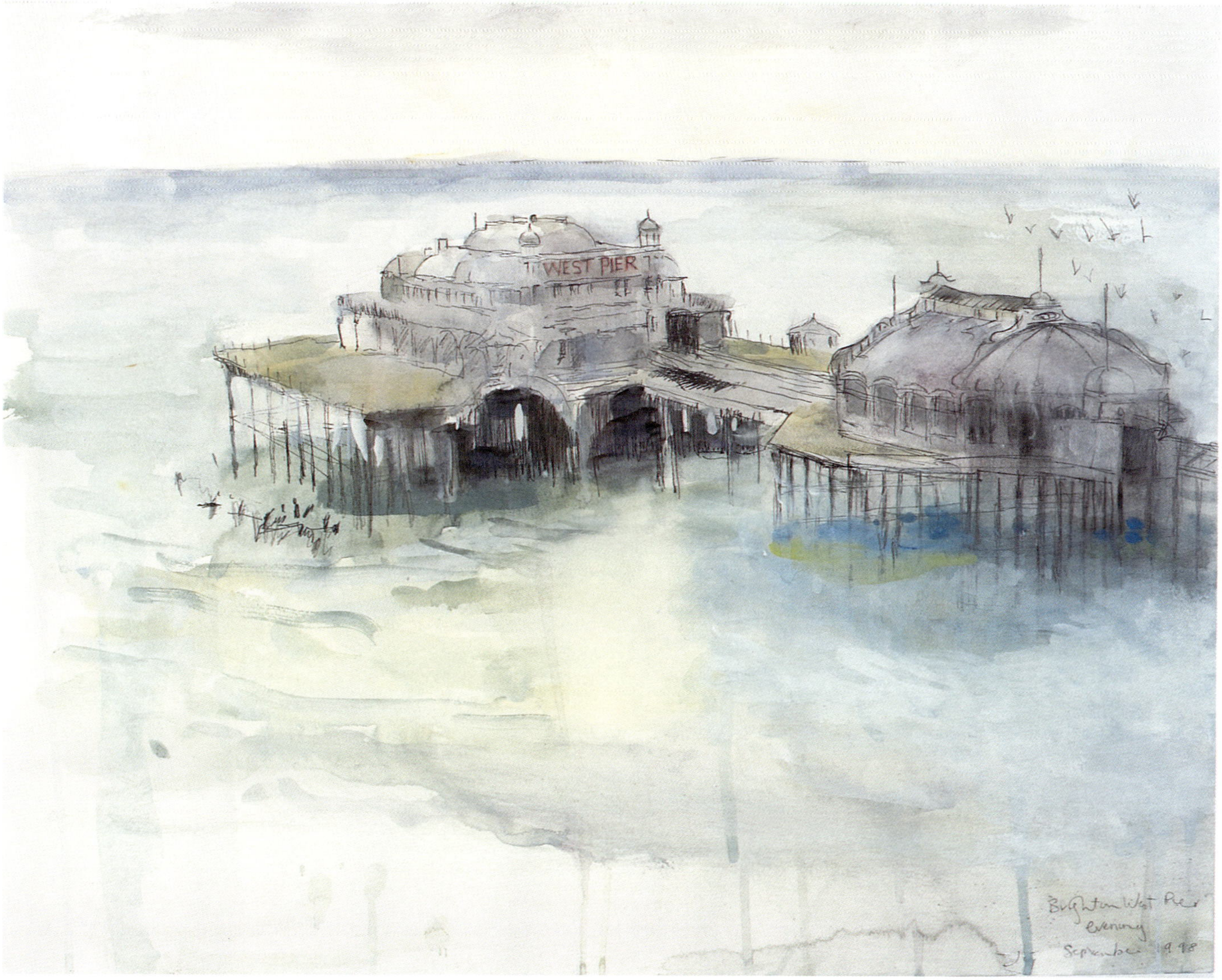

Brighton: sketch of West Pier in evening.

building. It was extremely well run, with pleasant and efficient staff. My large bedroom had two big windows, with a fine view of one side of the pier: exactly what I had asked for in my booking, and immediately we opened the bedroom door I 'saw' my first painting. The wind was blowing, the sea was rough and a wonderful emerald green, and as the waves smashed against the structure of the pier one could see just how vulnerable it was. I started painting at once. I had brought with me two very large sheets of a hot press, hand-made paper, and I got one out and pinned it on to the equally large piece of hardboard that I had cut especially to fit that size of paper.

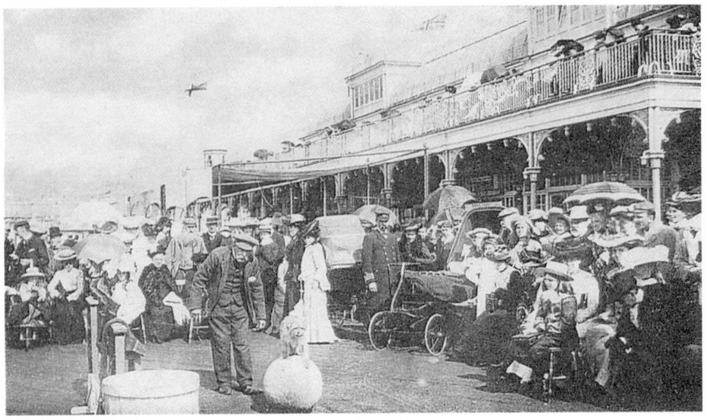

Entertainment on Brighton's West Pier, 1905.

Starting a picture that you have 'seen' is always exciting. I use a very fine pencil, perhaps a 2H, and get the composition in roughly and always impatiently, for at such times I long for the swiftness of a camera. With some of the drawing in, I put in the sky, but sometimes before that I put a pale colour wash over the whole drawing and as soon as that is dry, I am away – working flat out. 'Get something down,' 'Get something down,' I say, and then you can work on it, putting in, taking out, altering, but hanging on, for dear life, to your original vision, and trying not to lose sight of that.

I worked on that picture for two days. Then the weather changed, and it was calm, and very early in the morning the pier looked wonderful, like an Indian palace set in a tranquil sea. I did a little sketch of it, and got out my precious last, large sheet of paper and started drawing. The rising sun gilded the tired old structure, which no longer looked broken, but fresh, new, magical, glistening, with the sea and the sky surrounding it. No horizon was visible but just a glorious pale blue, pale pink dawn. The early mornings that week were heaven, and I felt a part of it all: just me, the pier and the wonderful sea and sky.

During the middle of those days we walked through Brighton, visiting the art gallery with its good Camden Town paintings, going round the Prince Regent's wonderful ornate pavilion mostly designed by his favourite architect, John Nash in 1815, and on Sunday morning we climbed the hill to St Nicholas, the parish church of Brighton and after the service we were invited to take coffee at the church with members of the Liberal Democrat Pary, who were holding their annual conference in Brighton. The street leading to the church had a row of delicious Regency terrace houses, white stucco and very

CLEVEDON

My next pier after Brighton's West Pier was to be Clevedon, the best surviving pier without buildings and listed as Grade II*. It was designed by R.J. Ward and J.W. Grover and built in 1868. It stands a good deal higher above the sea than most piers, and derives its grace from the supports on which it rests and the lacy ironwork in the spandrels between them. On May 23rd, 1998, Clevedon Pier was re-opened. 'A day to remember,' read the headline in the local *Mercury* as the small north Somerset resort came to life, thousands turning out to witness the grand re-opening of their pier. For all those years they had fought to see the town's prime asset restored to its former glory, slim though this prospect had often seemed. I had wanted to see the pier again, and to attempt a painting of it.

After its official opening in 1869, Clevedon Pier enjoyed a fairly trouble-free life until one fateful day in October, 1970, when a routine load-bearing test had to be carried out for insurance purposes. Not only did the test confirm suspicions that the elegant wrought-iron substructure had become unsafe, but it caused two of the pier's spans at the seaward end to tumble and collapse into the Bristol Channel. The pier head and its buildings were left standing like a forlorn island.

Distraught local residents formed a 'Save our Pier' campaign, which was formalised into the Clevedon Pier Preservation Trust. For some time the prospects looked bleak. With inflation, further damage to the remaining structure and growing scepticism, the pier seemed doomed to complete demolition. The poet John Betjeman made a tape recording in praise of the pier, comparing its elegant outline to 'a Whistler oil sketch or a Japanese print', the local council handed the pier over to the preservation trust, and National Heritage Memorial Fund and English Heritage both gave substantial grant-aid towards restoration work, which began in 1985.

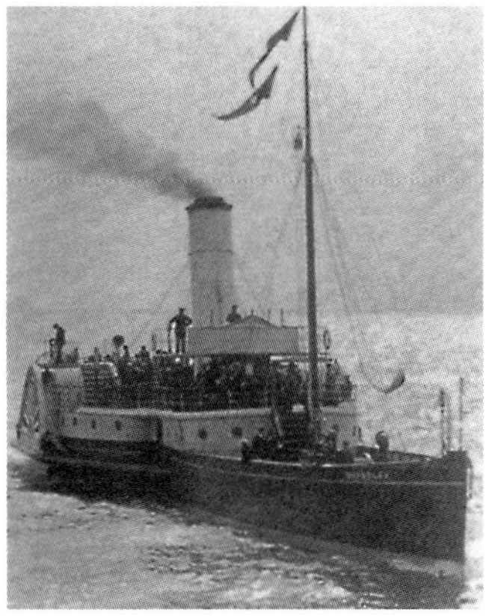
The paddle steamer *Waverley*.

On May 23rd, 1998 all was ready and Sir Charles Elton, who lived in nearby Clevedon Court, and who was the great-great-grandson of the chairman of the original Clevedon Pier Company, declared the pier open. The first to walk along the restored pier were those due to join the 11.30 a.m. sailing of the paddle steamer *Waverley*. The boat cruised the bay and the passengers also had a view of the newly restored Penarth Pier on the other side of the Bristol Channel.

From here, my childhood memories take over, for I had a friend, Anne Fry, who lived at Wotton-under-Edge when we had a cottage nearby at Kingswood. Her mother had been a Campbell, whose family owned the paddle-steamer company of that name. They plyed their boats down the Bristol Channel as far as Ilfracombe. The Frys lived, then, in a house on a sort of wooden platform over a large lake and we used to feed the huge trout there before diving in and swimming among them, but the paddle-steamers were what I longed to see, to be invited to go on.

I was determined to see it all again and to paint the newly restored pier. The muddy waters of the Bristol Channel were all mixed up with my childhood. In the school holidays, I would get the bus from Bristol to Clevedon. I was then fifteen, at boarding-school in north Devon. The family of my first boy-friend lived in a large, long white house in a narrow valley at Clevedon with the family firm of Hales Cakes on the opposite side of the valley. John Hale was at Uppingham and would write to me once a week at school and send me books. In the holidays I would go over and play tennis with him and afterwards swim in their pool, and he would drive me home in his little MG. It is sixty years ago, but I still remember how John's elder sister, Mary, always made me feel a completely unsophisticated child. After leaving school, John went up to Cambridge to read medicine. We lost touch and the next thing I heard, after at the age of nineteen I had married an Army doctor, was that John had been killed at Arnhem.

So the little Victorian town of Clevedon became associated with sadness. Indeed, it has always seemed to me a rather melancholy place of hard, grey stone houses. The poet I love above all others is Lord Alfred Tennyson and his *In Memoriam*, written ten years after his beloved Hallam's death in September, 1833, always seems to me hauntingly sad. Afterwards, he wrote 'It must be remembered that this is a poem, not an actual biography. It is founded on our friendship, on the engagement of Arthur Hallam to my sister, on his sudden death in Vienna, just before the time fixed for their marriage, and on his burial at Clevedon Church.'

On going to Clevedon to paint the pier I had so wanted to visit the church and to see Hallam's grave, and the memorials to John and his family, for his father had died of cancer when I knew them, and I remember vividly stooping down to kiss him as he lay dying, a very sweet man.

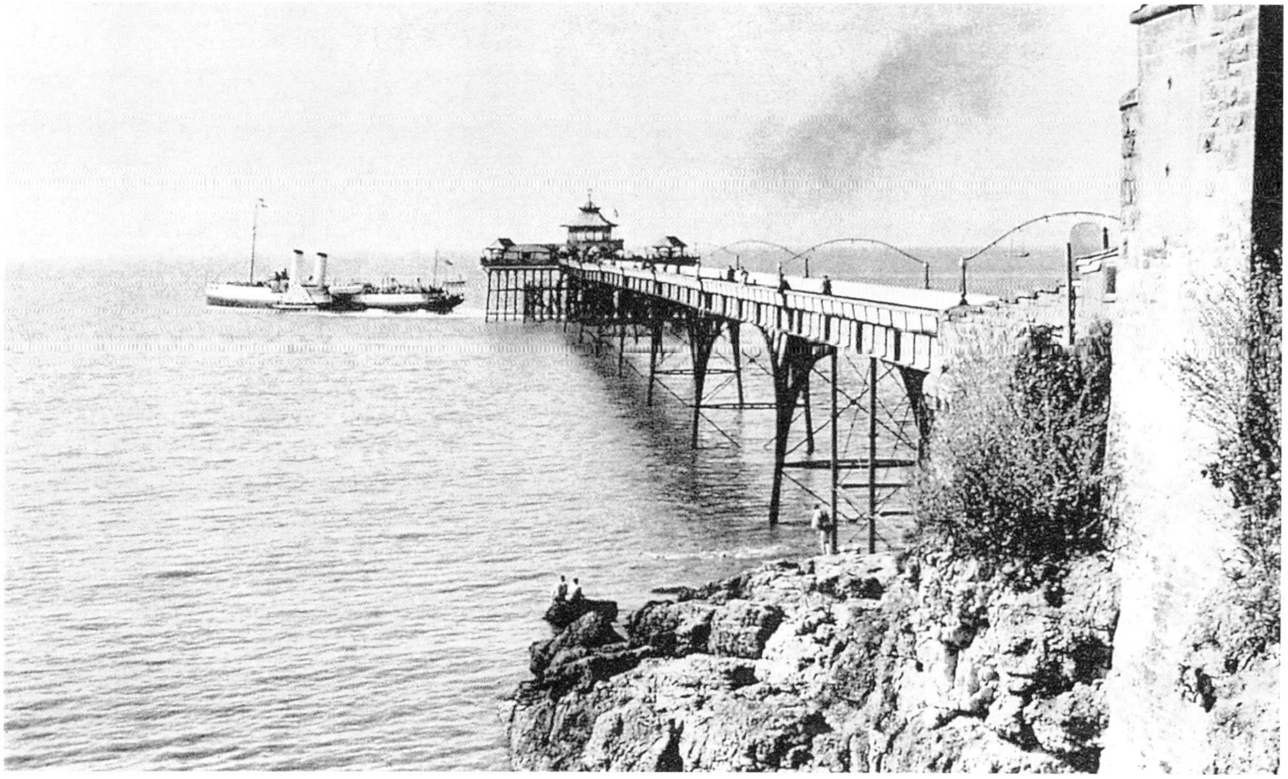

Clevedon Pier, 1948.

I tried to find a hotel to stay in; indeed I had booked one with a view of the pier, and with the same name as my house here in Henley – it sounded really promising – but just before I put the phone down the landlady said, 'Oh, by the way, I should tell you that we lock the house at 12.30 and do not open again until 4.30.' I said, 'Could I be locked in my room to paint?' but she was adamant. No guests were allowed in the house when she was out. I thought about it all day and then telephoned and cancelled the booking. And I just had a day in Clevedon to paint – no time to see anything else, no time at all – so I will have to go again: go again to visit the church and to remember Hallam, to remember the Hales and my childhood.

I think my watercolour drawing has caught something of the pier and of the brown and muddy waters of the Bristol Channel that as a girl I always wanted to be blue – the brown water and the grey stone buildings and the great river Severn flowing into the Bristol Channel. I looked and looked at it, and did my drawing, and took a photograph, and finished it at home; it had been a cold and sunless day in May and if I had stayed longer I could have got so much more done.

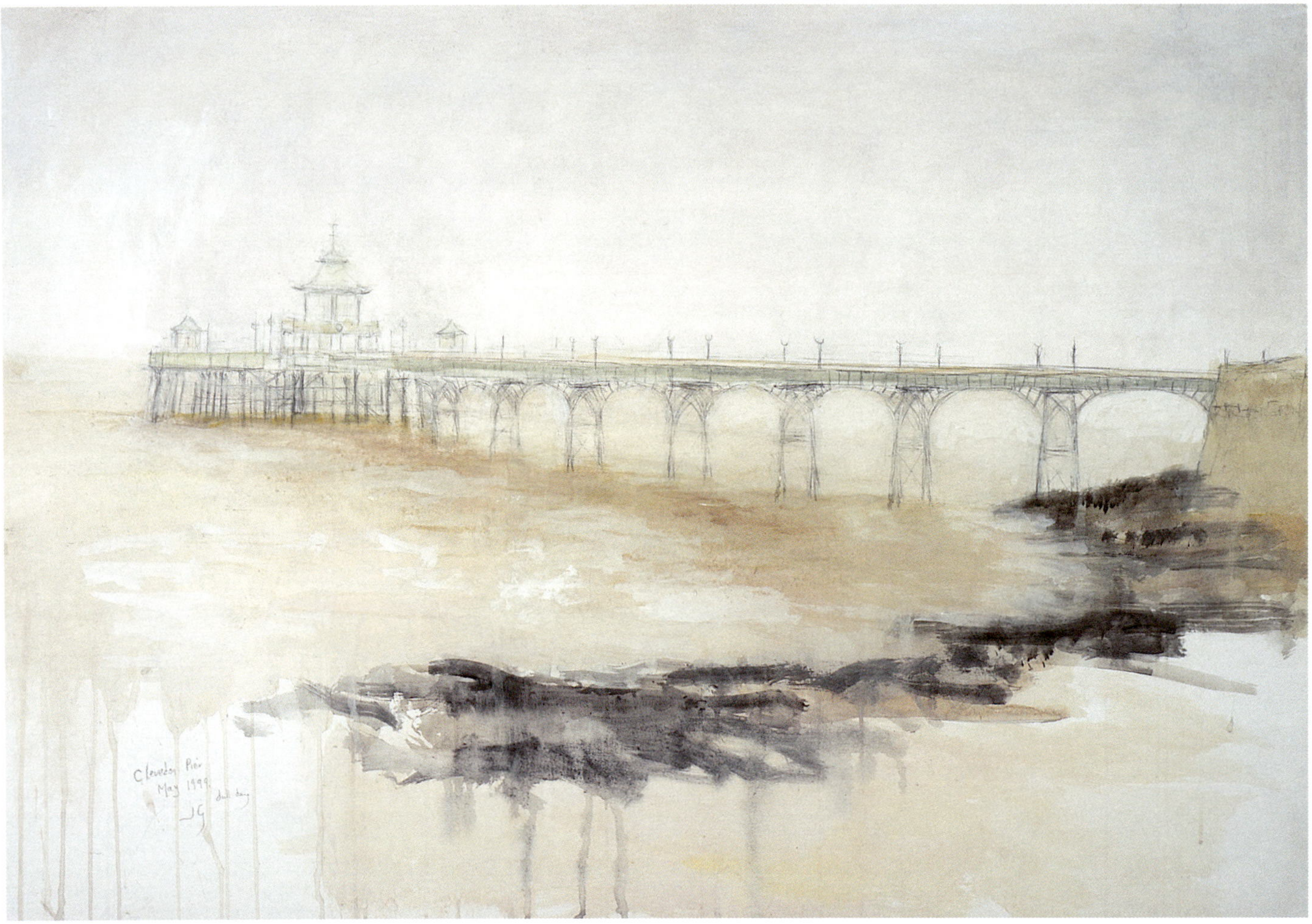

Clevedon Pier, early May.

Last night, thinking about Clevedon and about Tennyson, I sat up till 2.30 reading *In Memoriam* for the umpteenth time and found this poem that I didn't remember, number XIX, in the Christopher Ricks's edition of *The Poems of Tennyson*:

The Danube to the Severn gave
  The darkened heart that beat no more;
  They laid him by the pleasant shore,
And in the hearing of the wave.

There twice a day the Severn fills;
  The salt sea-water passes by,
  And hushes half the babbling Wye,
And makes a silence in the hills.

The Wye is hushed nor moved along,
  And hushed my deepest grief of all,
  When filled with tears that cannot fall,
I brim with sorrow drowning song.

The tide flows down, the wave again
  Is vocal in its wooded wall;
  My deeper anguish also falls,
And I can speak a little then.

And now I read that the landing stage for boats to the pier had to be built on three different levels in order to cope with the Bristol Channel tides, the second highest in the world. But Hallam's body had no landing stage to bring it safely to the shore. The pier had not been thought of then, but I seem to remember that at low tide there is a sort of slipway. Perhaps a small boat could draw alongside and Hallam's coffin be brought home.

TENBY

After leaving Clevedon we drove to the new Severn Bridge. I can remember when there was no bridge at all and one had to go up to Gloucester to cross the river by road. Now there are two bridges. But I do remember what fun it was to drive to Aust and cross over to Chepstow on the car ferry; that was like a great open-sided raft, and we thought it hilarious when the car belonging to a friend of my father's rolled off the ferry and sank in mid-river! Crossing the new bridge was lovely; the tall thin, sloping struts were a wonderful emerald green, making an exciting painting if one could only stop the car in the middle of the road to paint it. In the days when there wasn't much traffic I frequently used my car in search of landscapes to paint, and would stop, wherever I was, and climb out to sit on the roof to paint. One day my husband saw me doing this, and forever forbade it, saying I would cause a crash, with the car behind me coming out and hitting the oncoming car that had its view blocked completely by me.

I cannot remember anything particular about our drive to the end of Pembrokeshire and to Tenby, but we found our hotel quite easily. It was a flat-faced house, part of a terrace, facing the North Beach and built about 1820. We were shown our room and on going straight to the window – for it was the view from there that I was most interested in – I found that because it was flat and facing straight out to sea I could see nothing that I had anticipated of the bay or of the town. I said, 'Haven't you got a bay window or a window sticking out, or a room with a balcony?' The extremely pleasant proprietor said that the next room might suit me better as it had a balcony and, indeed, from the balcony I could see the most perfect view of the whole of the harbour from the point, right round to the church, almost to where we were, in a great smooth curve, a long flat picture – exactly what I wanted. Before unpacking I said to the kind, long suffering friend who had driven me there, 'Can we go straight off to find a builder's merchants who will cut me a large length of hardboard to put my biggest sheets of paper on? Can we go now?'

The builder's merchants were just closing and I said, 'Can you cut me a board 55 inches by 25 inches?' They said they couldn't as they hadn't got an electric saw! I couldn't believe my ears. They said that I would have to order it beforehand. Luckily, a very pleasant chap hearing this conversation and noticing my anxiety said, 'I'll do it for you and do it right away, with a sharp hand-saw.' As he cuts, we talk.

are probably Tenby's most famous citizens, certainly its most exciting ones. There was also an exhibition of local amateur artists and a very pleasant woman asked if we would like to visit her at home the next day to meet some of them. It wasn't actually in Tenby, and because I had so little time to paint, we couldn't accept.

Each afternoon we looked at something new, exploring the terrace and saw a plaque on one recording that Nina Hamnett the painter had been born there. When I was an art student, Nina Hamnett was still a well known name. In 1932 she had written the first part of her memoirs, *Laughing Torso*. I remember reading it avidly, but I cannot remember ever having seen any of her paintings. As it happens, the Tenby Museum had held a centenary show of her work in 1990. In 1955, the year before she died, she produced the second part of her autobiography, *Is She a Lady?* but I have never be able to find it, and no-one seems even to have heard of it – not even the owner of the interesting little antiquarian bookshop in Tenby. It was there that, to my joy, I found a lovely book of Augustus John drawings, rather a fine limited edition, with an original lithograph, a self-portrait, as the frontispiece. It was fairly expensive, and looking at it at leisure, back home after leaving Tenby, I notice there were only 49 drawings instead of the listed 50. At some point in the book's history, someone, I am sure, had been sold one as an original Augustus John!

Our visit to Tenby was fun and I got one quite interesting painting out of it, but a week is never enough. Both Turner and Girtin had travelled through that part of Pembrokeshire, Turner in 1795 when he was quite young and doing his topographical scenes; his sketch book of some sixteen drawings around Tenby is in the British Museum. How much more difficult travelling must have been then, but somehow they had more time. I had to finish my big watercolour and my dear faithful companion drove me home, and I would wait till September to go to the sea again to paint – next time, I hoped, to Cromer, for I had always longed to go there and I knew it had a pier.

CROMER

Cromer Pier has had a rough history. A jetty 210 feet long was built in 1822 but was washed away in 1843, to be replaced two years later by a structure 30 feet longer than the original. This lasted until 1897 when it, too, was destroyed by high seas. In 1900 a 500-foot iron pier was designed by Douglass and Arnott; they were both the designers and engineers. Alfred Thorne was the contractor, it cost £17,000 and opened on June 8th, 1901. A bandstand was erected at the pier-head and was extended in 1905 to support a pavilion. This seaward pavilion continues to stage traditional summer-season variety shows and Sunday concerts. Beyond the pavilion, on the seaward side is the very modern life-boat house and launching ramp. In spite of constant exposure to the elements, the pier is still in good condition.

Without the opportunity to reconnoitre a place it is difficult to know where to stay, where to find a hotel with a view from its windows that would make a good painting. I started my research by telephoning the manager of Cromer Pier. He was extremely pleasant and helpful, and told me the name of a guest house on the front with a good view of the pier and added, rather amusingly, that it had just been repainted. I had the name of the house and the owner, but he didn't know the telephone number. I rang telephone enquiries, only to be told after a long wait that the guest house was not connected to the exchange. A strange guest house, I thought. After consulting various guide books and the AA Guide, I sent off to the Red Lion Hotel for a brochure and I knew immediately, on opening the envelope, that this was where I wanted to stay. The cover of the brochure had a photograph of the old town from the beach; it looked exactly what I was looking for, a view that would inspire me and that I could paint with pleasure. I telephoned at once and booked a room with a bay window looking out to sea. I booked it for a week in September.

Carol, who had nursed me back to health after my accident, and who had come with me to paint the West Pier at Brighton, would accompany me to Cromer. Mr Hobbs, our local retired undertaker, who often drove me, would take us across England to East Anglia and the North Sea. We were now all set. It seemed, somehow, a very long drive, but when we arrived, there was no doubt in my mind at all that this was where I wanted to be. The old part of Cromer was lovely, and lived up to the picture on the brochure. The Red Lion Hotel, a

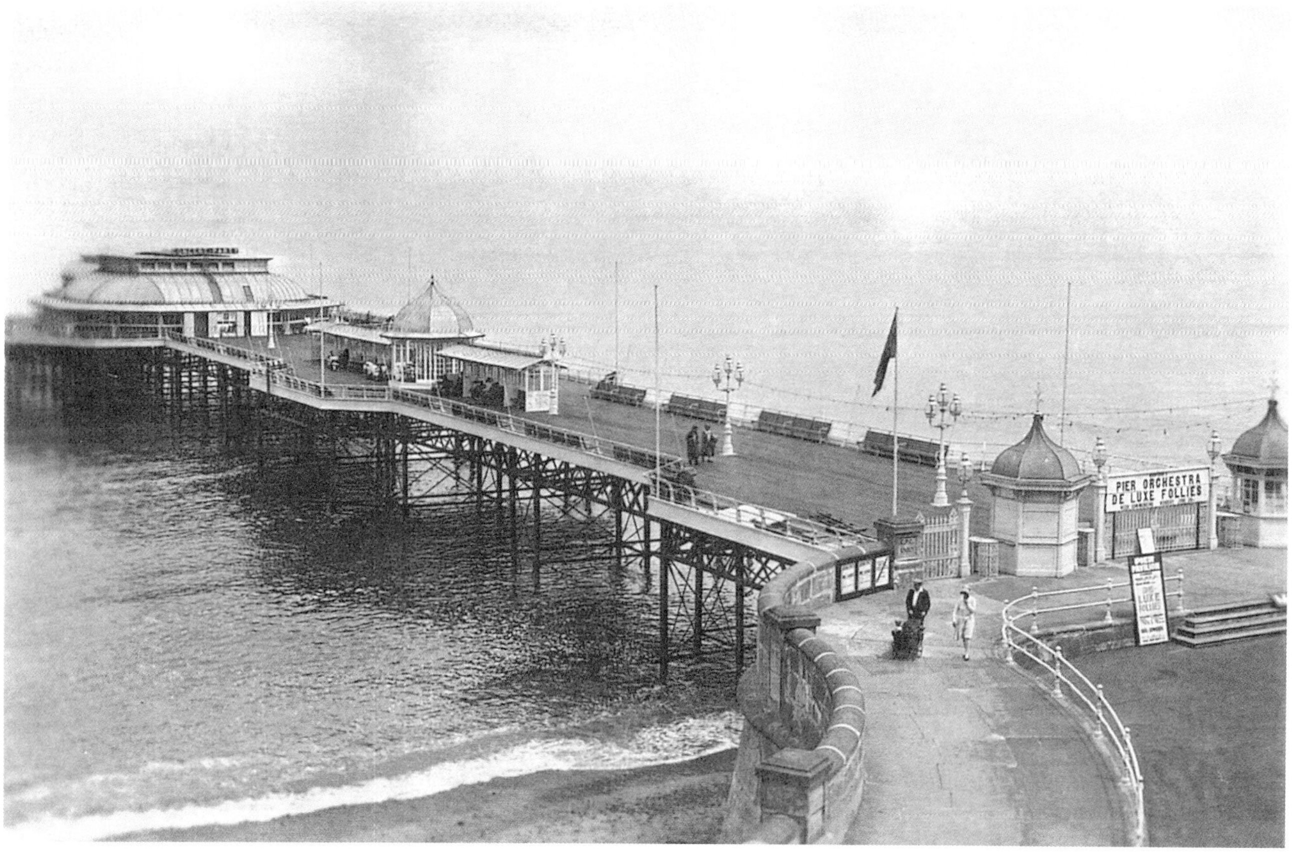

Cromer Pier, 1932, when the entertainment included the pier orchestra and 'de luxe follies'.

red-brick Victorian pub, was just right. It faced on to a curved terrace with seats placed round it, and from where there was a very good view of the pier. The view of the pier from the hotel itself was half blocked by a tall, grey building, which looked like a rather shabby rooming house, for we could see directly into a sad and derelict bathroom from our bedroom window.

Our cases and my painting clobber were taken to our room, large, pleasantly old-fashioned with windows facing north and east. Stairs are now a problem for me, but these were wide and shallow and the old polished mahogany bannister on one side and my walking stick on the other made it possible. Carol carried my paint-box and paper when I wanted to go down to paint.

On our first night, we went down to the dark panelled dining room. It was very pleasant, but no-one else was dining. An elderly waitress came for our order, the menu looked interesting, but quite expensive. We ordered, and when the waitress came back with our

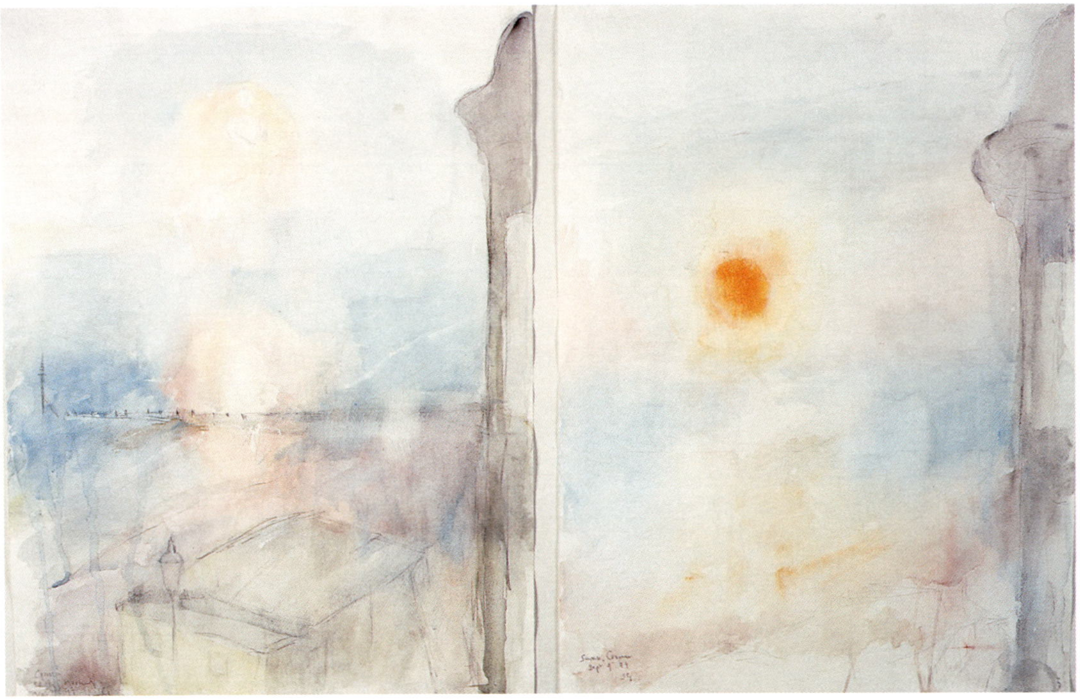

Cromer: two views of sun rising over the sea.

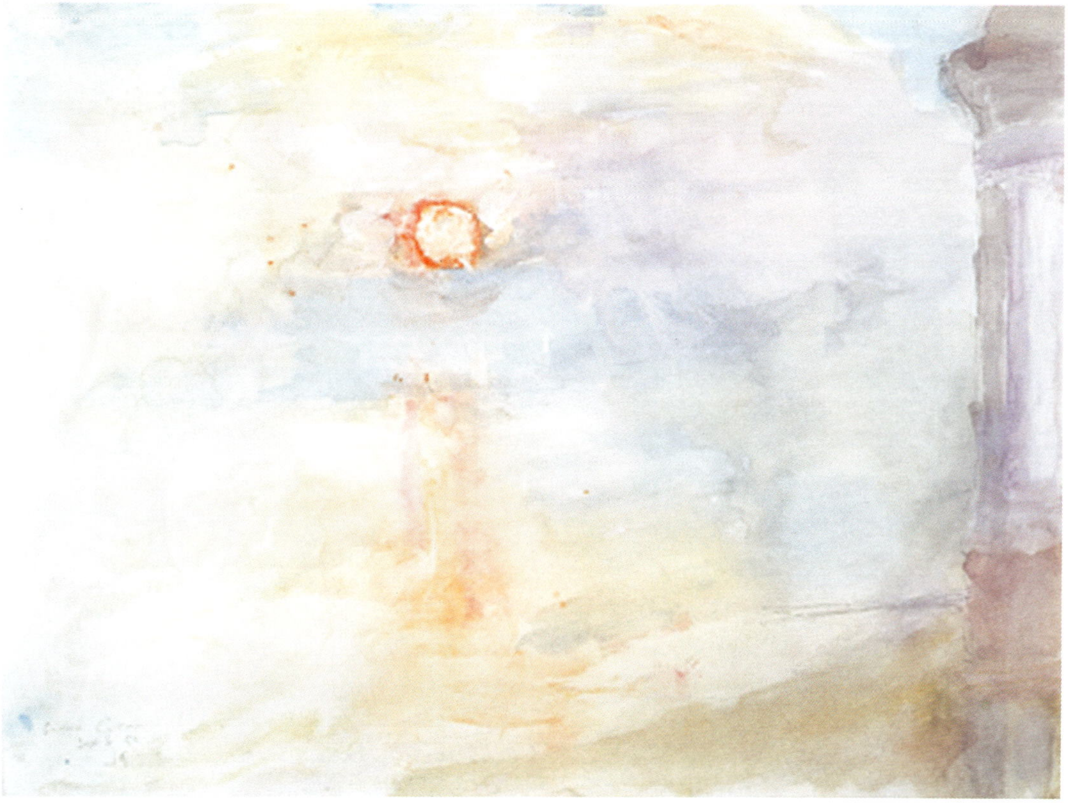

Cromer: sunrise over the sea.

first course, we talked to her. She was dressed in the traditional black dress, white frilled apron and white cuffs, the correct dining room uniform for centuries, hardly altered. 'Do tell me why we are the only people eating in the dining room, surely there are other people staying in the hotel?' I said. She looked at me, with a twinkling eye, and said, 'Oh, it's much too expensive for the people who come here. If you want to eat, the bar is much better.' So after that we followed her advice and ate in the bar, where indeed we had some excellent sea food and good company, and we saw our waitress and the dining room only for breakfast.

My bedroom window faced due east, and waking very early in the mornings and looking out over the sea, I was able for the first time in my life to watch, and to paint, the sun rising up over the water. I did this on four mornings, light watercolour sketches, which I had intended to work up later but then I decided to leave them as they were: just a faint memory, each sunrise being quite different, but magical.

In order to paint the pier I had to go outside and sit on the curved bench on the terrace, Carol carrying my painting things down, my paint-box, sheets of paper and a large bottle of water. As I so often find, my sheets of paper were not long enough but at least my boards were and so, with my beloved paper clips holding everything together, I managed to complete two paintings of the pier. While I was working on them a charming elderly woman came to sit beside me to watch, and after a little while she got up to go, saying as she left, 'You've really caught our pier there. I would recognize it anywhere.'

With great difficulty and with Carol carrying everything, I managed to walk down the ramp that the crab boats used, to get to the beach so that I could look back to the hotel, could look back to that part of the old town, with the tall church tower of St Peter and St Paul. The 160-foot tower, by far the tallest parish church tower in the whole of Norfolk, watching over it all. I could not manage the dozens of steps going down to the beach that lay below us, but the ramp was much easier and the beach was so lovely that the effort was worth it, for the view looking back was really exciting. Looking up to the end of Brunswick Terrace I noticed a beautiful, curved eighteenth-century house that I fell in love with and could imagine living in: high up over the sea with a wonderful view, wonderful for painting the wild north-

WESTON-SUPER-MARE

My next seaside, my next pier, would be Weston-super-Mare where we went so often as children – where we used to be turned out on the beach in freezing weather because it was 'good' for us, and where, as a child of seven or eight, I would go alone for half a mile or so walking over the sands to Uphill. In the sand dunes there I had chanced upon a dead dog, and I felt sorry for it, and would go and see it every time I was on the beach, watching, horrified, as it got more and more bloated. With each visit it became more terrifying and I never dared to tell anybody, but could not keep away.

Now I was going back to Weston to paint the old pier, the Birnbeck. The foundation stone of this Eugenius Birch-designed pier was laid in 1864 and it opened on June 5th, 1867. It was a 1,040-foot cantilevered construction to the rocky Birnbeck Island and a short jetty extending westwards from this island. In 1872 improvements included the 250-foot wooden north jetty, and in 1881 a lifeboat station was built (the boat-house being added in 1889). Not until 1884 did they build the first pavilion with a tramline that would transport luggage from the paddle steamers when they docked at the jetty. Sadly, on Boxing Day in 1897 a fire badly damaged the main pier buildings and the following year a new pavilion was built. In 1902 they decided to rebuild the lifeboat station.

Over the years the pier suffered much from gales and serious neglect, but it stayed open and was used spasmodically until, eventually, it was thought best to shut it down. In 1941, during the war years, the Admiralty took it over and used it until 1946, when it was known as HMS *Birnbeck*. From 1962–1972 the steamer company, P & A Campbell Ltd ran the pier until they sold it to John Critchley, a year after their regular passenger steamer services ceased to call.

John Critchley tried to establish a restaurant on the Island and, having some contact with the Welsh National Opera and Nell Moody, who with her husband John had helped to establish the opera company in Wales, he decided to ask if she could organise a group of young opera singers to perform in the dining room and entertain his guests. My opera-singing son, Nicholas, was at that time studying with Nell Moody. He once took me to meet her at her house in Clifton. He was then only 19 or so, and she tapped his chest affectionately and said, 'A great future there, our own Boris Godunov, for he has a fine bass voice.' One evening, we drove some ninety miles to have dinner in the new restaurant and to hear Nick sing, but the restaurant did not last long, and once again the pier was up for sale. I heard it had now been bought by someone who has won the National Lottery.

In late December, 1999, after collecting my large double portrait of my youngest son Toby and his wife from the Royal West of England Academy exhibition in Bristol, I persuaded Mr Hobbs to drive me to Weston-super-Mare. It was a cold, grey, wet day as we drove slowly along the front while I tried to 'see' a painting. I had nearly given up and despaired of ever finding what I wanted when we came to the old Royal Pier Hotel (where I had stayed with my father in 1936) and there was the Birnbeck Pier, lapped by a wild grey sea, and a painting waiting to be done. I went straight in to the sad old hotel, desperately in need of a coat of paint, and I booked a room, there and then, facing the Birnbeck Pier for the beginning of April.

Now April was here, and my niece Deborah was to accompany me, and excitedly I waited to see if my painting was still there. And I thought of the great Norwich School painter, Cotman, who on his way to a dinner party 'saw' a painting, tied up his horse, and arrived at the party six hours late. Paintings do not always wait. Would this one? I always think that one should get something down immediately and never wait, whatever the circumstances, but this is very difficult, for so often others are involved.

We were driving to Weston on the motorway in a blizzard, the snow settling on the road verges, the wipers struggling to keep the windscreen clear. It was the coldest day of the year. The once grand Royal Pier Hotel (Royal because Queen Victoria stayed there and was able to bathe her feet in a specially constructed pool of sea water) is built out on a rock virtually in the sea, the only hotel in Weston not cut off from the sea by a dual carriage-way with appalling traffic, civic gardens and a wide promenade. We were shown to our bedroom, a large pleasant room but to see the pier one had to stand right up to the window, and then there was only a slanted view of it. The window was permanently shut so that even to lean out was impossible. I complained and eventually we were moved to another room with a permanently sealed glass door that

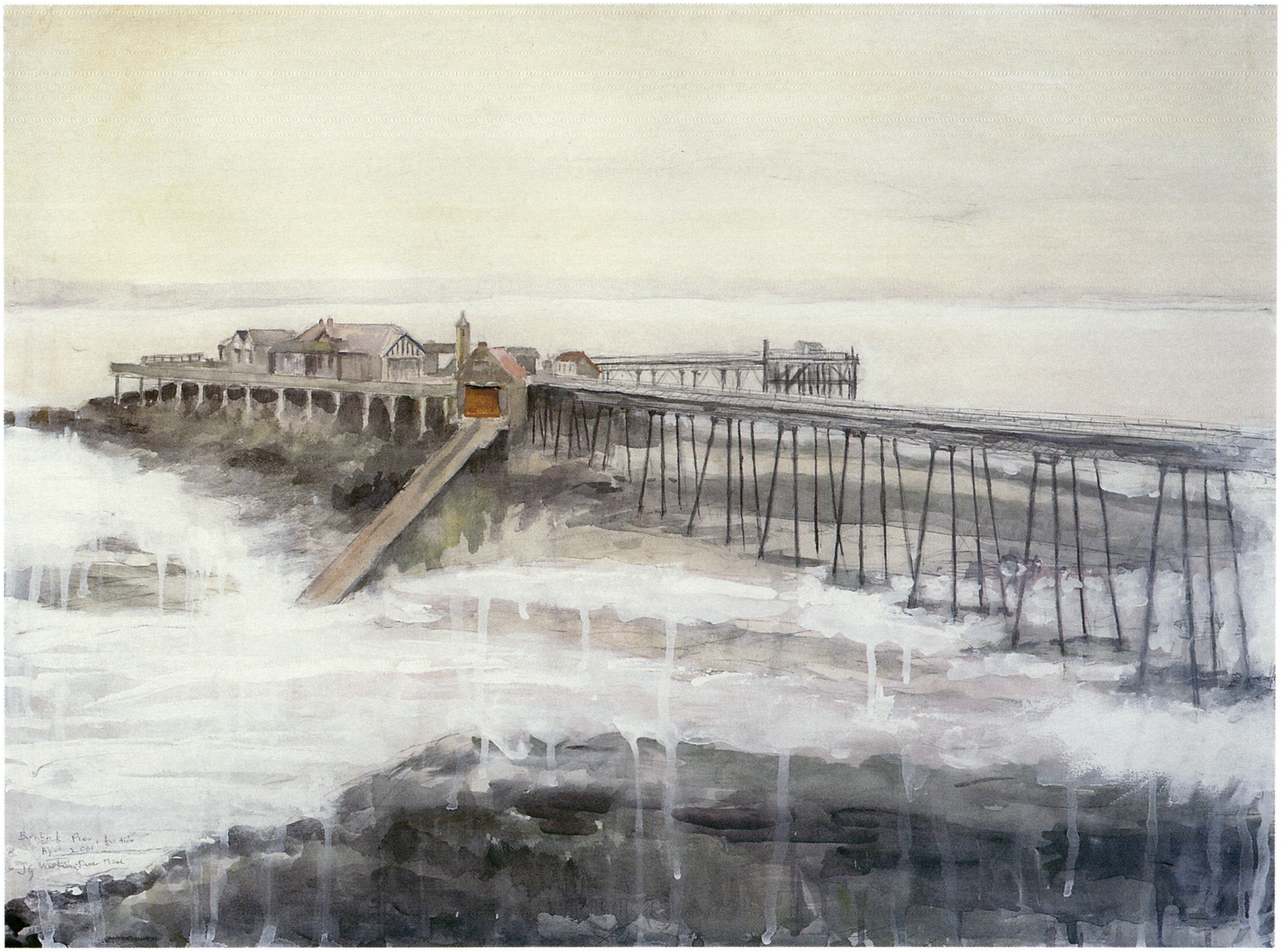

Weston-super-Mare: Birnbeck Pier, evening at low tide.

had once led on to a balcony. The balcony was now a complete wreck and boarded up, but the view of the pier from the glass door was perfect. You could see most of it, for the room projected from the main face of the building, built at an angle with nothing obstructing its view. It was the only bedroom in the hotel to actually face the pier.

It was then too late to start painting, so I began setting up my easel for the next day. In front of the glass door onto the balcony there stood a very heavy old trouser press, difficult to move, so instead of moving it, I tried propping up my drawing board and paper on it. I found, to my amusement, that it made a perfectly adequate painting easel that held my board securely at the right height, for I prefer to paint standing up. There was no need to move anything and I could begin painting as soon as I liked. Does anyone actually still use a trouser press to press trousers?

Next morning the tide was high, the water lapping the cast iron stanchions of the pier. It was not the painting I had seen in December, for the sea was now a chocolate brown, with an incredibly high level of mud suspended in the water making it completely opaque. The sky was a dark blue and snow lay on the top of the Welsh hills over the water behind Cardiff. The pier was sad, derelict, abandoned. It had not, after all, been bought by a lottery winner, and it had very little chance of being restored for all the available money had already been spent on the 1930's art deco fun pier on the esplanade. The only sign of life was the lifeboat house with its red doors and its ramp down to the muddy sea. The general public were forbidden access, the gates locked and barred. The pier had been derelict for ten years; perhaps in a few years' time all that will be left will be my painting of it. It's a very sad thought.

On that first morning, I got in the foundations of a painting. The tide was very high, the sea brown: there was a painting there, if only I could get it. I had forgotten that the tides of the Bristol Channel had such a high rise and fall and that the seascape would change completely in a few hours; so that in the evening I had to start quite another painting of it, this time at very low tide. It was extremely interesting, the rocks, the stanchions of the pier, the sea and the pale sky, the weather now much calmer. I look at it now, having spent time working on it, and think it quite exciting, a

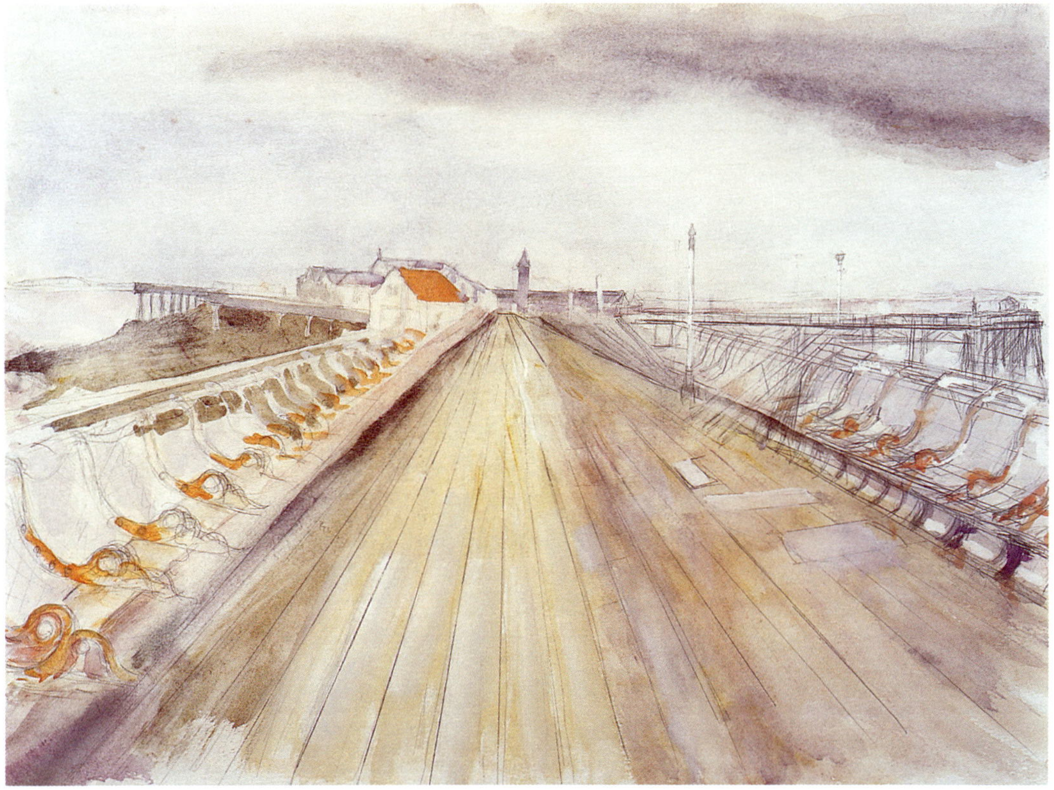

Weston-super-Mare: looking back along ruined deck of Birnbeck Pier.

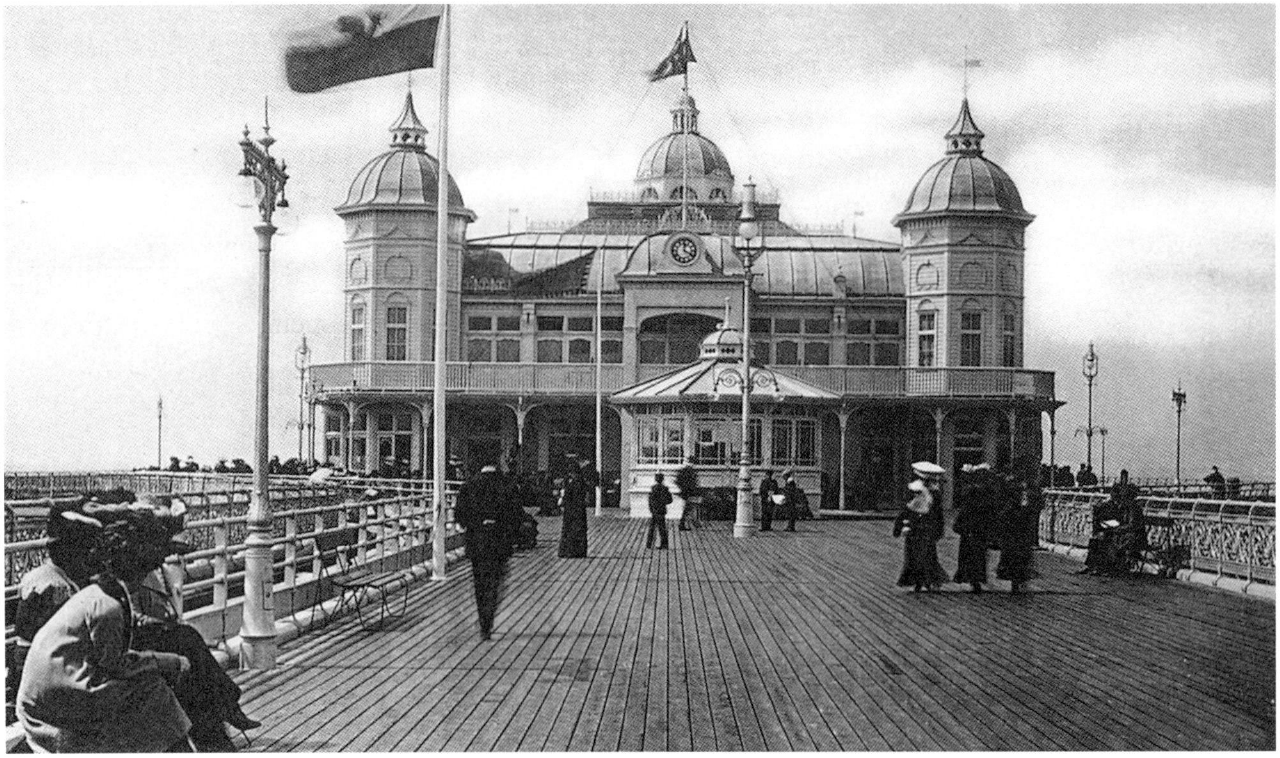

Grand Pier, Weston-super-Mare, 1908.

One of the family stories I have never been able to live down concerns that stay there with my father in 1936. His Royal Highness, Haile Selassie, the deposed Emperor of Abyssinia, was also staying in the hotel with his family and his court, for they were living in exile in Bath, after Mussolini had invaded and conquered their country. I well remember his small, very dignified figure, his ramrod-straight back and the sad expression on his noble face.

I was in those days a very keen swimmer and every day would run to the newly opened art deco swimming pool on the front, where I would dive in without a bathing cap and in the skimpiest of bathing suits. I would swim a few lengths of the bath, get out, and then dive back in again. Being very thin and very sunburnt, my thick black hair wild and wet, I would run back, bare-foot, to the hotel. One day, on this run, I was stopped by a journalist and a photographer from the local newspaper who asked if I was the daughter of the Emperor of Abyssinia! I thought this rather an honour, but the others found it hilarious and I was teased relentlessly . . .

Now in April 2000 I had nearly finished two paintings of Weston's Birnbeck Pier and thought that perhaps I should try and get a sketch of the Grand Pier, for it was considered Weston's premier pier and had been given all the available National Lottery money, really because it was the 'fun pier' situated in the centre of the esplanade and therefore likely to be popular with visitors to the town.

Plans for the second pier date back to 1880, but work did not start until November 1903 to the design of P. Munroe. It opened on June 11th, 1904, and measured 1,080 feet and cost some £120,000. It included a 2,000-seat pavilion, and was intended as a home for opera, music-hall, Shakespearean plays, ballet and boxing matches. By 1906, a 1,500-foot low-water extension with a timber landing stage had been completed but the hazardous conditions meant that few boats ever moored there. So, apart from 120 feet beyond the pavilion, the extension was demolished between 1916 and 1918. Light amusements were added in 1926 but in January, 1930 the pavilion was totalled destroyed by fire.

It was the greatest peace-time fire in Weston's history, and deprived the town of visits from some of the country's finest entertainers, including the Carl Rosa and D'Oyly Carte opera companies.

In 1932 it was rebuilt in the art deco style and housed a large fun-fair instead of a theatre. The pier changed hands just after the Second World War, but nothing of significance happened until 1970 when the entrance was rebuilt, and in 1974 the pier was granted listed building consent. A new bowling alley was added and approximately £350,000 was spent on re-decking and installing a two-storey Fun House.

This huge white structure at the end of a long and featureless walkway made it a difficult painting to compose, and it was only on our last day there that I caught a paintable glimpse of it across the bay, which is the sketch I reproduce here. Given time, I could have made a reasonable painting of it, and it would have been fun doing it.

I had heard from Jean McKinney, our recently retired Secretary at the Royal West of England Academy, of which I am an academician, that in Bristol City Art Gallery there is a painting of piers by a painter called Peter Mathews, so on our way home we called in to see it. It was like a chart of architectural drawings of thirteen south-coast piers, each drawing perhaps five inches deep and some twelve inches long, all hung vertically side by side and mounted on a single sheet of paper, making quite a big glazed picture. It was not remotely like what I was trying to do with my pier paintings, quite another view, but an interesting one.

So now I have painted Weston's piers and, in June, I plan to go to Blackpool, a town completely unknown to me, but with three piers and the North Pier originally designed by the great Eugenius Birch. We shall see! I look forward to it with interest and some trepidation.

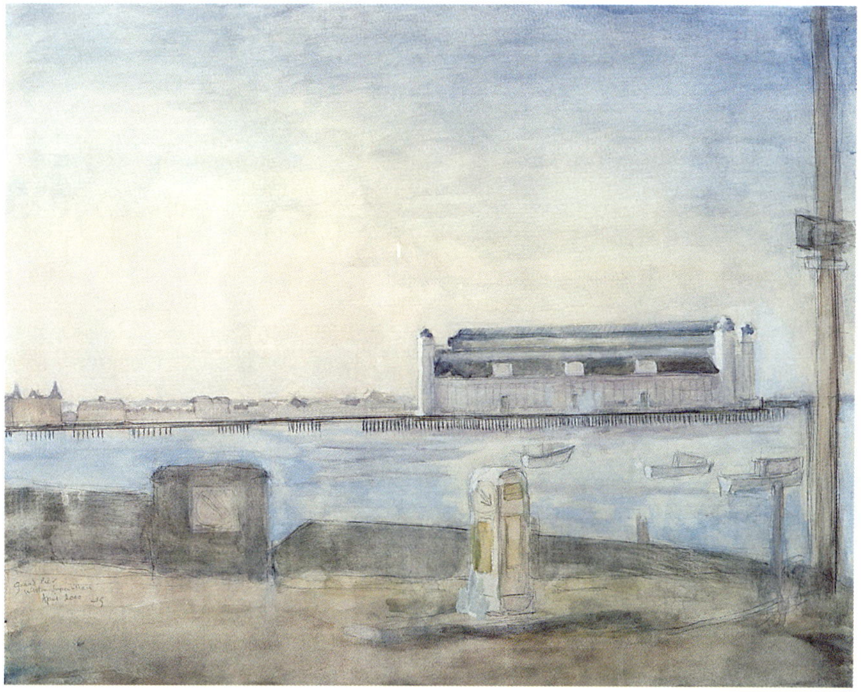

Weston-super-Mare: sketch of Grand Pier across the bay.

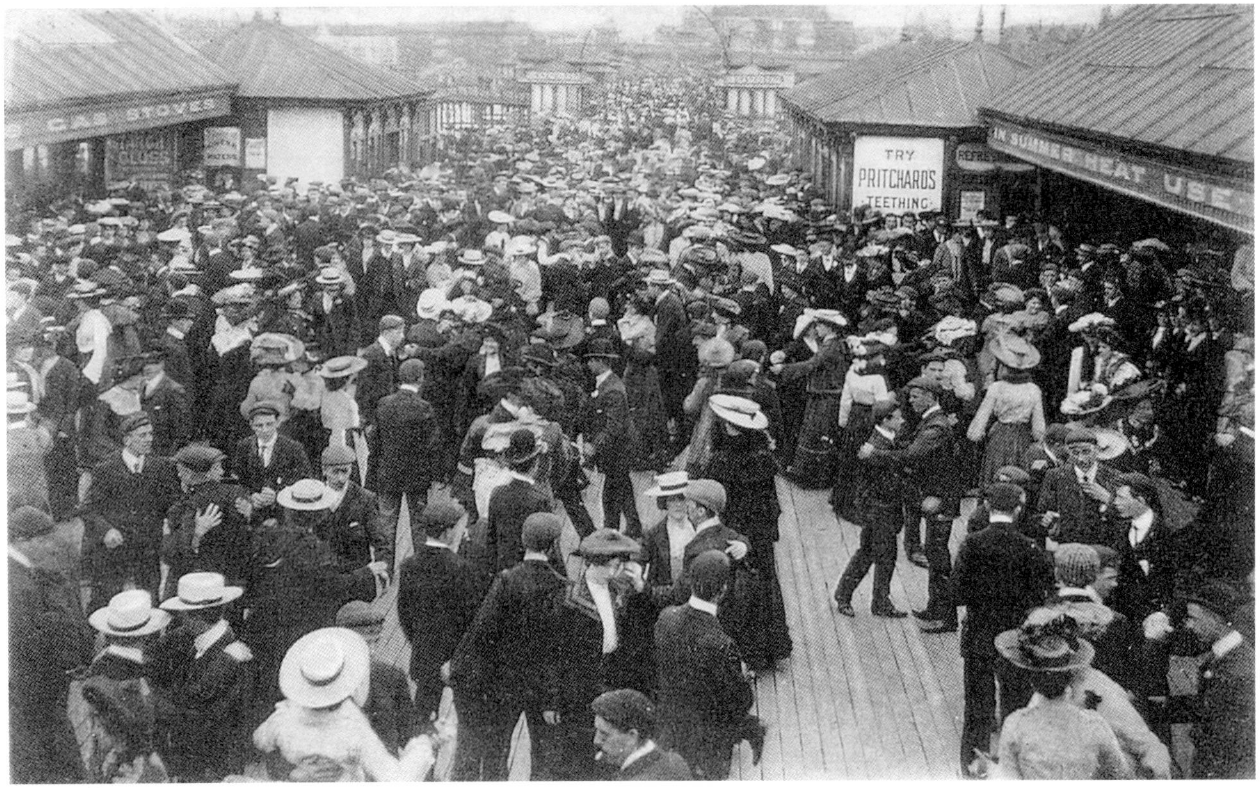

Dancing on the Central Pier, Blackpool, 1906.

AND FINALLY TO BLACKPOOL

Whenever I go to a new place I buy a Pevsner *Buildings of England* for that area, so I now have a Pevsner for North Lancashire. The entry on Blackpool begins unpromisingly: 'The Ministry of Housing and Local Government has issued no list for Blackpool, which means there are no buildings of architectural or historic interest in the town'. But then I am interested in painting piers, and I see that the North Pier, a view of which I hope to have from my hotel window, was opened in 1863, the Central Pier was built in 1868 and the South Pier opened on Good Friday, 1893. Although they have all been damaged by fire, storms and rebuilding, something must remain, and the splendid idea of a structure going right out into the sea is always interesting. My map reading tells me that Blackpool must face west and so, perhaps, I will be able to get some paintings of the sun setting over the sea to go with those of Cromer, where I had such fun trying to paint the sun rising.

We arrived in Blackpool after a long and tedious motorway drive. Coming off the motorway, the outskirts of Blackpool seemed to go on for ever and I wondered who lived there, and why. Curiously enough, I have just read an article in *The Times* on George Carman, one of the most famous of our contemporary barristers, which mentions that he was brought up in a suburban house in the outskirts of Blackpool.

As we neared the coast, the houses became larger and started to display 'bed and breakfast' signs, and then red-brick villas took over with hotel signs in their front gardens. At long last there was a sign to the Tower and the Promenade and, to my joy, I caught a glimpse of a simple elegant pier with little kiosks on it. We arrived at our hotel, The Clifton, which seemed to be built on a road island. At the desk a friendly and pleasant girl checked our bookings and a helpful porter dealt with our suitcases and my endless painting boards and sheets of paper, heavy paint-box and easel. The weather was like November, the sea rough and grey, the bedroom I was shown to was austere, with a bathroom like a dark cave, but the view of the pier was superb, just what I had asked for.

As I watched, the yellow-grey sea receded and beautiful golden sands appeared, and there was a painting there to be caught. I got out a large sheet of hot press paper, put it on a board, put up my easel and started painting. It was exciting. The bedroom was stuffy, the windows would not open, so I called down for the hotel porter. He came, produced a screwdriver, as the windows had been screwed shut. Now they would open, but I realised the problem, for I was nearly blown away. It was June and the weather was wild, not a soul about. Blackpool, the main resort of the north-west was quite, quite empty.

The North Pier, the only one of Blackpool's three piers to remain virtually unspoilt, was built by Eugenius Birch in 1862. Birch, an imaginative and inspired engineer, was commissioned by the Blackpool Pier Company Ltd. The company met in the Clifton Hotel, Talbot Square (the hotel in which we were now staying) in 1861, when the leading townspeople discussed the possibility of erecting a pier for 'the greater promenading space of the most invigorating kind'.

To this end, they wished to erect 'a substantial and safe means for visitors to walk over the sea to a distance of some thirteen hundred and fifty feet at high water'. Twenty eminent men subscribed the preliminary expenses of forming a company which was started with capital of £12,000 in 2,400 shares of £5 each. The first pile was placed in June 1862, and the pier was opened just under a year later on May 21st, 1863. The *Illustrated London News* of May 30th carried a full report of the proceedings. 'From an early hour in the morning, the trains, both ordinary and special, discharged large numbers of visitors, and by noon, when the proceedings of the day may be said to have commenced, the number of strangers was little short of 20,000.' The newspaper continued:

> The appearance of the town itself was as gay as any holiday could make it. Streamers, flags and banners almost hid the thoroughfares, the shops were closed, and everyone appeared to join in the festivities. The pier and its immediate vicinity formed the great point of attraction. The ceremony of opening the Pier began with a Procession, which represented all the local interests of the town. The marching of the procession occupied about two hours and, after passing through the chief streets and round the Pier, it halted opposite the Clifton Arms Hotel, where Mr F. Preston, the Chairman of the Pier Company, said that the pleasing duty devolved upon him, on behalf of the Directors of the Blackpool Pier Company, formally to open the undertaking which they had commenced last year. The crowd gave several hearty cheers, and the demonstration was increased by a salvo of artillery . . .
>
> A dejeuner was afterwards served in the Clifton Hotel, to which about 150 persons sat down. Mr Preston occupied the chair, and

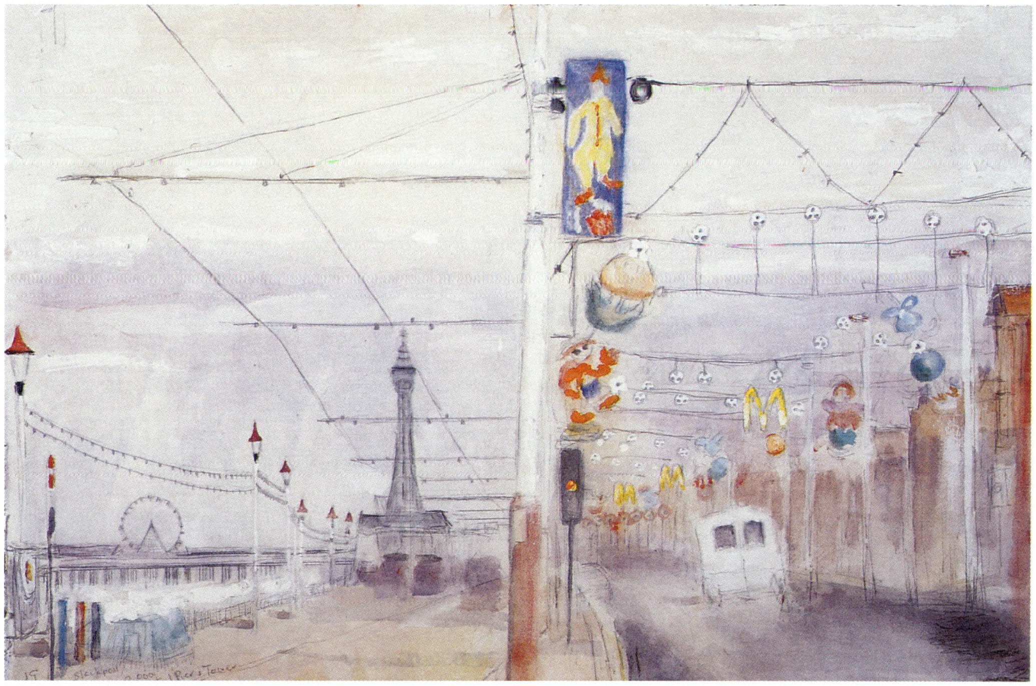

Blackpool: Central Pier, the Tower and Ferris Wheel painted from the Promenade, showing preparations for the autumn illuminations.

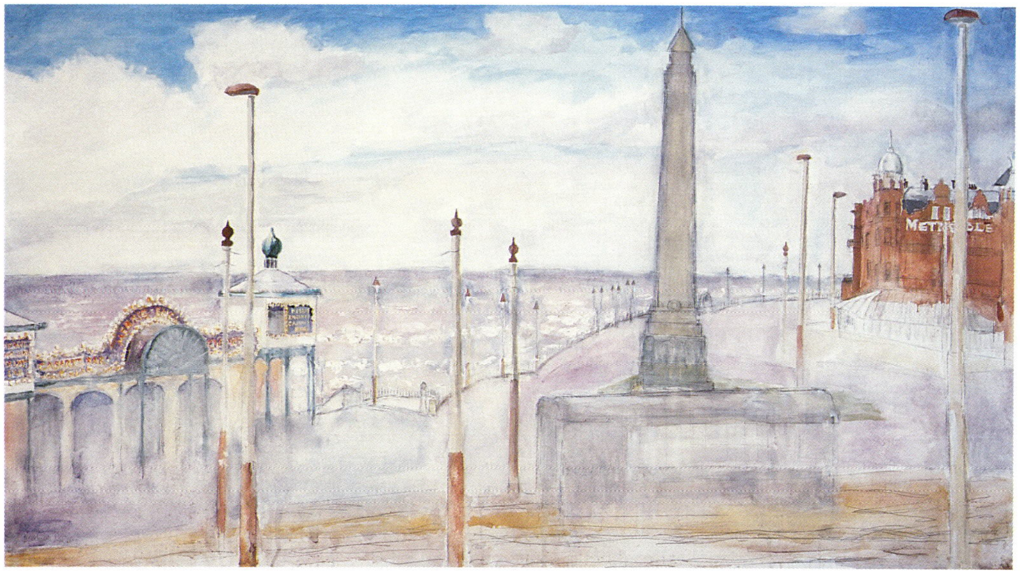

Entrance to North Pier, with the War Memorial and Metropole Hotel, very stormy sea in background.

after a few speeches from him and other gentlemen, the proceedings terminated.

The North Pier acquired its first pavilion in 1874 under the name of the 'Indian Pavilion'. Its concerts became famous throughout the country, and attracted the attention of eminent critics. Orchestral music of the highest order was performed there, and Edward de Jong was conductor of the Pier Orchestra. De Jong was the most eminent flautist of his day and in 1883 Simon Speelman followed him as conductor; later in his career, he became an eminent viola player with the Hallé Orchestra and the Brodsky Quartet.

In the 1890s, Blackpool welcomed over three million visitors a year and pier accommodation was on a correspondingly grand scale. The North Pier, greatly extended in the 1860s, was further extended in 1875 and in 1877 with the addition of north and south wings on the pier head; this area then measured one and a half acres. Electric light followed and the pier was widened in 1896-97, practically doubling its size. A photograph from 1912 shows the North Pier absolutely packed solid with people.

In 1921 fire destroyed the 'Indian Pavilion' and a replacement was opened in 1923 with seating for 1,500 people. A Mr Jacobs and his Rumanian Orchestra played selections from musical comedies. A memoir from Selwyn B. Allen in the *Blackpool Post and Gazette* in 1970 recalled an August week in the 1920s when the sun shone brightly and he escorted two girls from his 'digs' on to the pier; one of the girls felt there was romance in the air, for Mr Jacobs gave as an encore a piece he had just composed for a member of the audience – it was called 'Because of You' – but, alas, when he acknowledged the applause, the elegant lady had disappeared. But Mr Allen remembered the tune and the words:

The sunshine seems brighter because of you,
My sad heart is lighter, the sky more blue,
No dark clouds can gather where hearts beat true,
And love reigns forever because of you.

The pavilion suffered the same fate as its predecessors, and was burnt down in June, 1938. The present pavilion is a square white block.

I had hoped to have three Blackpool piers to paint, but the North Pier was the only one to remain comparatively unspoilt, the others covered in huts and amusement arcades, and the South Pier had a towering, crane-like 'bunjie jump' at the end. I did a watercolour sketch from the promenade of a bit of the Central Pier with its ferris wheel and the famous Tower nearby, and the decorations ready to be illuminated in the autumn when Blackpool is packed, with thousands of visitors coming just to see the lights.

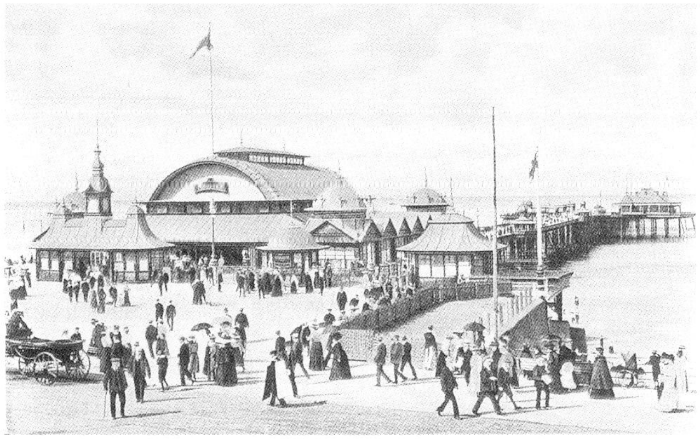

North Pier, Blackpool, 1904.

Looking round the hotel, which once had been rather grand, I found the first floor residents' bar, and looking out of the windows I visualised a really exciting painting: the edge of this painting formed by the entrance to the North Pier, with its Merrie England bar, the middle of the painting with the tall obelisk, Blackpool's war memorial, and the end of the painting, the large red-brick Metropole Hotel – these strong vertical shapes and Blackpool's streets lights and the tall pillars for the trams making a fascinating composition set against the stormy sea.

The hotel lift was out of order and the porter kindly carried my painting paraphernalia down from my second-floor bedroom so that I could set up my studio in the bar, having first obtained consent from the hotel manager. My hopes of painting the sun setting over the sea behind the North Pier were never realised, as there was thick cloud every evening we were there. My paintings of the sunrise at Cromer on the other side of the country will not have the companions I had planned.

In the end, I got four paintings: the North Pier painted from my bedroom window, one at low tide showing the golden sands and one at high tide with a very stormy sea; the entrance to the pier with the Metropole Hotel and the war memorial from the residents' bar, and a small painting of the Central Pier, the tower and the ferris wheel which I painted from further along the promenade.

I do, though, have another souvenir of Blackpool. I had an introduction to a charming man, Derek Carmen, who was the owner of a glorious stone-mason's yard: it was full of exciting things, Elizabethan chimneys, stone urns, and it was there that I found two beautiful old stone finials – large round stone balls with a double line etched round them, and each standing on a stone pedestal. I bought them and arranged for them to be sent down to Henley by carrier, and they now stand on each side of the end of my garden path. In the early mornings I stroke them lovingly; they lead to a corner of my little

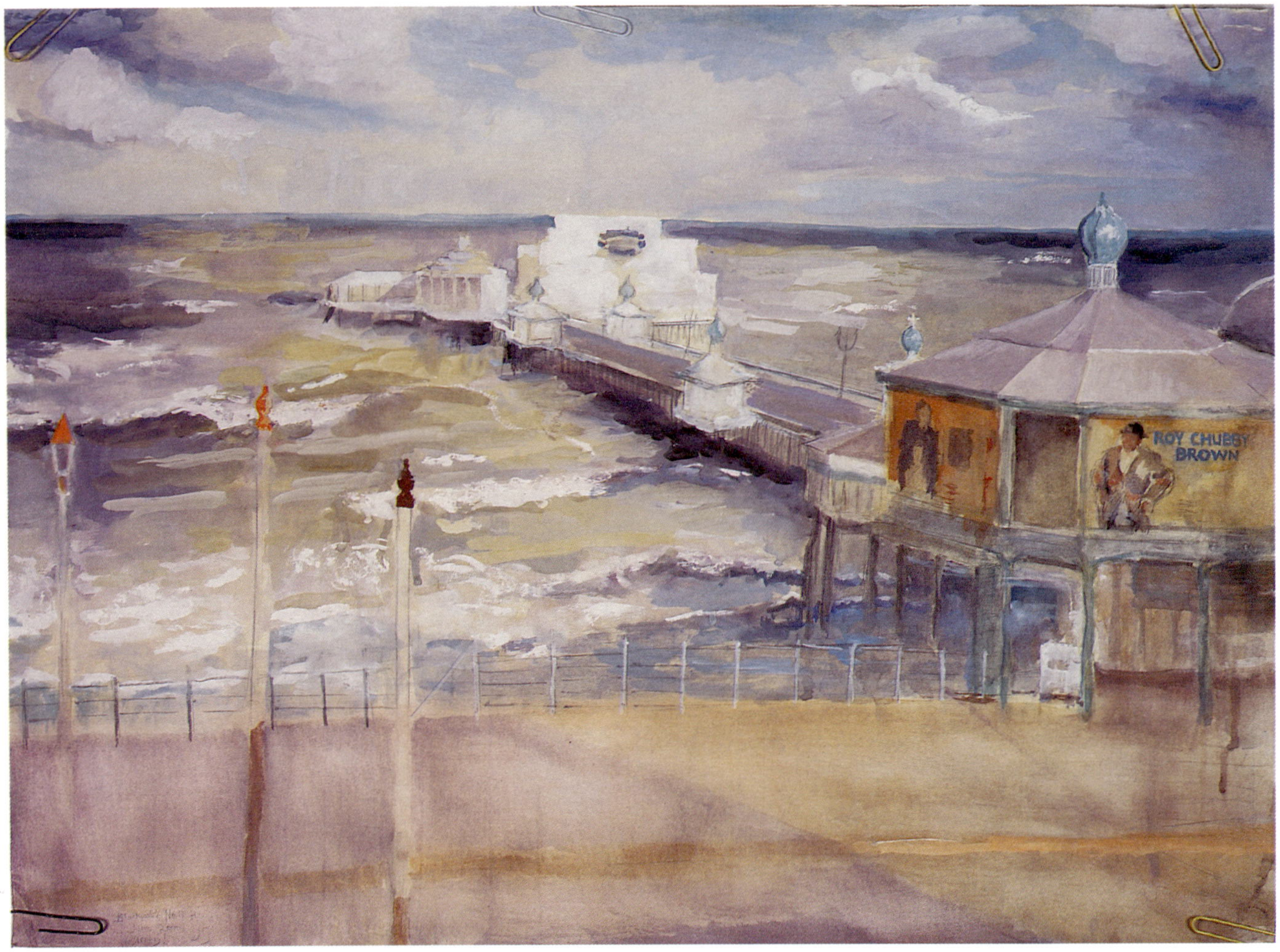

Blackpool: North Pier, high tide and very strong sea.

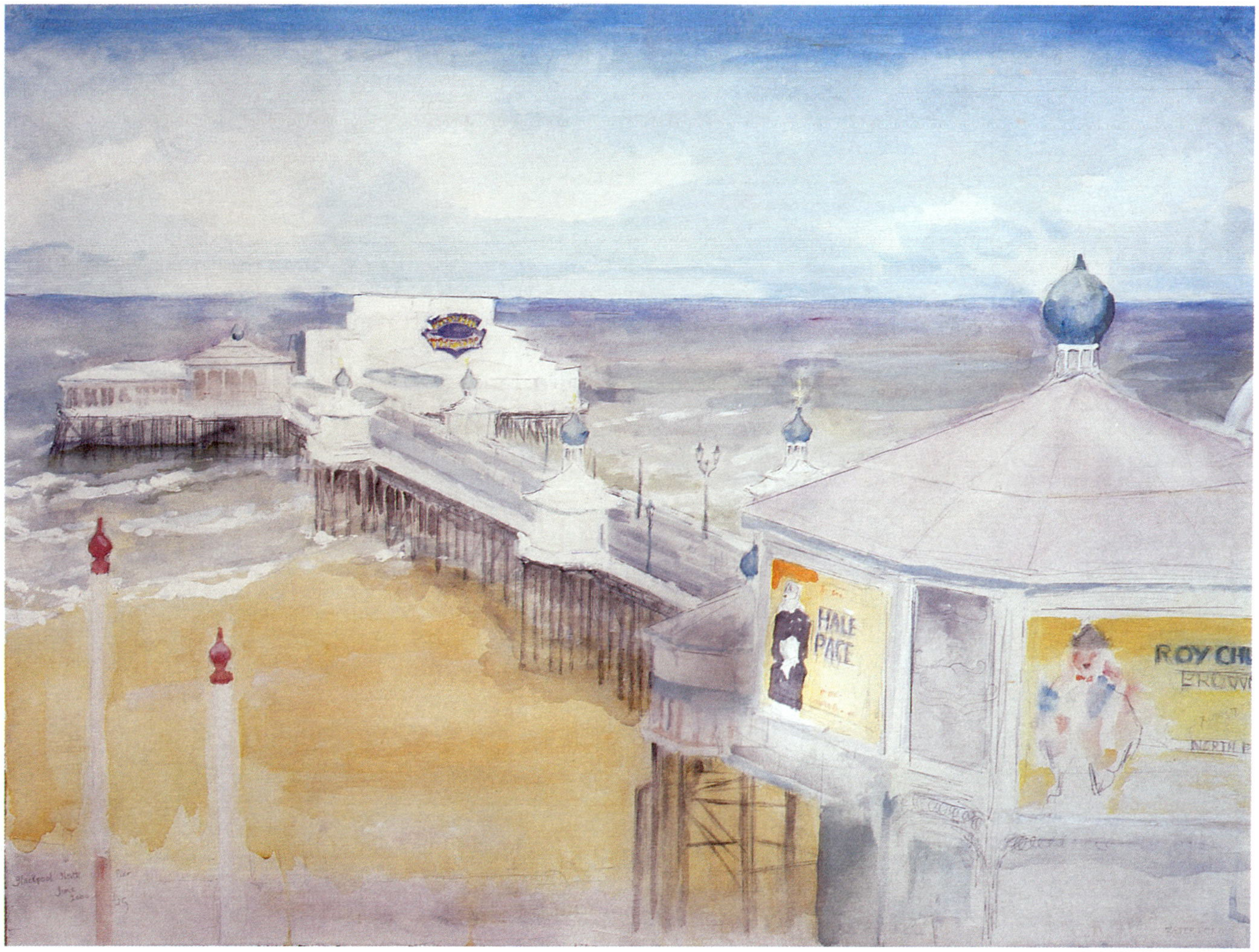

Blackpool: North Pier, low tide revealing golden sands.

town garden where I can sit and watch the sun rise in the east, completely unobserved. A grand but simple pleasure.

I have come to the end of my journeys to the sea to paint piers and seaside towns. It has become increasingly difficult to find piers that have not been spoilt; and increasingly difficult for me to get to them. I have painted some fifty paintings for an exhibition and for this book to go with it, and it has all been the greatest fun, giving me an exciting project to carry out which I have really loved doing.

Sadly, in our age of cheap foreign travel with almost guaranteed good weather, people no longer go to the English seaside to enjoy the innocent pleasures of the traditional seaside and the amusements on the pier. These wonderful constructions striding out into the sea have become something of an anachronism; that, and the fact that they were built of cast-iron and have been constantly pounded by the waves and high winds and are now in great need of care and attention. Many piers were privately owned and with the prohibitive cost of restoration owners frequently took the easy way out, often demolishing them completely. Some now have hideous concrete buildings which ruin their wonderful silhouettes against the sea.

I have been privileged to paint some of the finest piers and to have recorded them on paper, at dawn and at dusk, and in different lights and at different times of the year. And it was splendid to be able to paint perhaps the greatest pier of them all: Brighton's magnificent West Pier, before its restoration. I hope I live to see that restored to all its former glory and to witness, perhaps, a resurgence of interest in piers and in our once great seaside towns which, thronged with people every summer, were once such an important part of the British tradition.

And yet, Matthew Parris writing about the West Pier in *The Times* has said:

> There was only ever one thing of beauty in Brighton, and they are about to destroy it.
>
> The Brighton Lanes are rather sweet, I suppose - as the French say, *curieux*. The Regency facades, like a thousand other Regency facades, are quite fine. The Grand Hotel is, in the nature of Grand Hotels, grand; and the Pavilion is as soulless and gaudy as any camp Arabian fantasy can expect to be.

> But nothing touches us; nothing moves the spirit; nothing stirs the memory . . . nothing, except the ruined West Pier: that 'drowning chandelier' of Hanif Kureishi's imagination. It was the most beautiful thing.
>
> And now they want to destroy it. Yes, *destroy*, for a ruin has the soul of a ruin, and to refurbish a ruin kills what there was and replaces it with something new.
>
> New and dead. New and yet utterly unoriginal. What will now rise upon the rusting stanchions and lurching cross-members of the wrecked West Pier will be a mixture of tart-up and replica. The intention is to make the structure look as it did 90 years ago. Isn't there enough in Britain that looks as it did 90 years ago? Heavens, that isn't even *old*: just a lifetime's span away. We shall gain one more neo-Victorian confection, and lose something unique: a sad and lovely ruin. We shall spend £30 million to kill something, and receive in its place a neat pile of artful tat.
>
> Because a ruin is, as we all are, dying . . .

Perhaps that is it. Perhaps he is right, I don't know. I don't know at all.

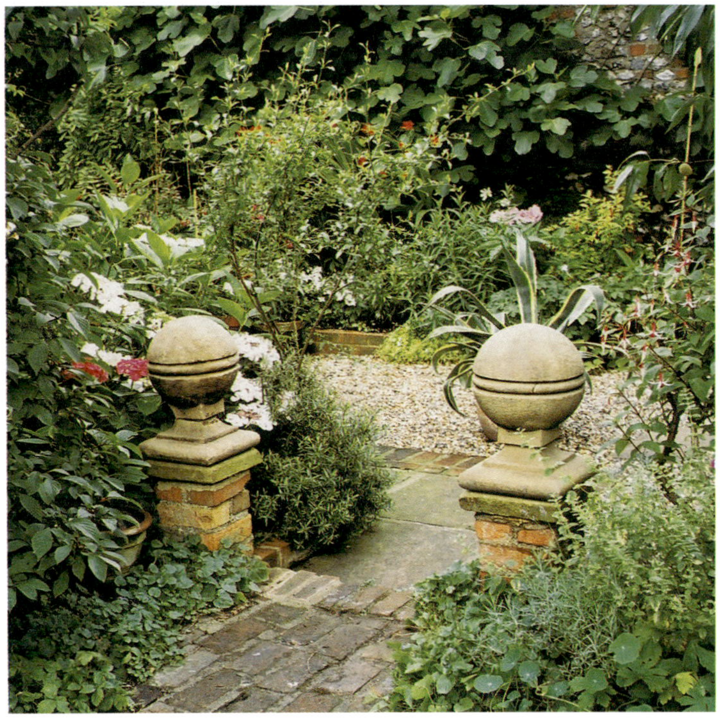

The stone finials from Blackpool, now adorning the author's garden path in Henley.

Index

Numbers in **bold** relate to illustrations

NATIONAL PIERS SOCIETY

The National Piers Society was founded in 1979 under Sir John Betjeman, at a time when some of the finest piers were threatened with demolition. Over the years the Society has grown steadily and is now established as the leading authority on piers. Through its efforts, several piers that would otherwise have vanished remain for the enjoyment of everyone.

The Society's aims are to promote and sustain interest in the preservation and continued enjoyment of seaside piers. It publishes a Guide to British Piers and a quarterly magazine, and advises heritage bodies, lottery boards, local authorities and the media on pier matters. It organises visits and talks and holds its annual general meeting in a different resort each year.

Honorary Secretary, National Piers Society: 4 Tyrell Road, Benfleet, Essex SS7 5DH
Tele: 01268 757291 Fax: 020 7483 1902